£1.50

RETURN VIA DUNKIRK

RETURN VIA DUNKIRK

by
GUN BUSTER

Windrow & Greene

© 1994 Windrow & Greene Ltd.

First published 1940 by
Hodder & Stoughton Ltd.

This edition published 1994 by
Windrow & Greene Ltd.
19A Floral Street
London WC2E 9DS

A CIP record for this book is
available from the British Library

ISBN 1 85915 095 0

Printed and bound in Great Britain by
Biddles Ltd, Guildford and King's Lynn

DEDICATED
to the
Officers and Men of Y–Battery,
whose courage, endurance, and
unflagging cheerfulness made
this book possible.

CONTENTS

PRELUDE TO BATTLE

BATTLE

CONTENTS

PRELUDE TO BATTLE

I—DEPARTURE

THE dear old house looked me full in the face over the' sparkling waters. There it was, perched on the green wooded hillside with the path straggling down to the pretty sandy beach. There it was, warm and mellow in the late afternoon sunshine, radiating peace and the peaceful virtues, very lovable, very English, and—which seemed most miraculous to me—unchanged.

Unchanged. Yes. And because of this I realised painfully what a complete and utter change had befallen me, The house was its old self even to the last brick, the last roof-tile, just as I had known it for at least twelve years. But I—— Well, I was on the deck of a crowded troopship anchored off the Island in Spithead, waiting for darkness before making a dash to France. I wore a tin hat to save my skull from being dented by shell splinters, and a life-saving jacket tied on with waist tapes in case I was torpedoed. I carried a gasmask and a gas-cape to save my eyes from being burnt out and my body from being horribly blistered, and a revolver in case I had to kill someone, and an identification bracelet in case I got killed myself.

I was panoplied for War.

And the dear old house was Peace—Peace as I had known it for so many years, with the long flow of happy hours, sunny gaiety, high-spirited young men, and laughing girls. Though its familiar windows looked straight at me across the dancing waters, I thought, " It could never recognise me now. I don't seem to belong to it any more."

I felt a slight pang. " Shall I ever belong to it again ? " I thought.

Suddenly I had a curious feeling of being without age, neither young nor old. Ageless. And only five weeks before I had known I was twenty-seven. Known it, so it seemed, very intensely, and borne the knowledge with much equanimity. And the dear old house had known it, too ; and in fact, had made no small fuss in celebrating it. Five short weeks before. And now ? Well, as I have said, I felt ageless.

Somebody came up and stood beside me as I leaned over the ship's rail. It was the Drag-Rope, otherwise L-Troop Leader of Y Battery in which I was Battery Captain. The Drag-Rope had been called up after being two years on the Reserve. In the interval he had married and become a father. Also, he knew the dear old house on the Island, and all it stood for, even better than I did.

So it is not surprising that we stood there together in silence, watching the soft grey walls become merely a shadow in the fading light, and finally a part of the blackness encompassing us. He knew what I was thinking, and I knew what he was thinking. And you, I expect, can guess. Near enough.

*   *   *   *   *

We had embarked at Southampton at midday. The War was only three weeks old, and the 2004th Field Regiment R.A., consisting of two 25-pounder batteries, twelve guns in each, was one of the first Territorial regiments ordered to France. Now that we were on the ship, and such things as embarkation leave had faded into the realms of the Impossible, we made a point of being proud of the honour. The Colonel, be it said, was proud without any reservations. When there was no point in being otherwise, and the

regiment had finally moved out of billets, it soon
became infected with a pride as lofty as the Colonel's.

Our guns and vehicles had already left England
from another port. We were to meet them again
" somewhere in France." That is, if they, or ourselves,
were not torpedoed on the way over. An artillery
regiment separated from its guns is like a fond mother
parted from her children. She isn't happy till she gets
them back. So it was with us. On the troopship we
missed their companionship. We felt we had lost
something. It didn't seem like home without them.
" Wonder how the guns are doing," became a common-
place expression to which no answer was expected.

There was a regiment of medium artillery (six-inch
howitzers) on board. They felt like us. Their guns
were also tossing about in the Bay of Biscay—or at
the bottom of the sea. We sustained each other with
words of entirely unfounded optimism.

It was four in the afternoon when the grey, shallow-
draught transport with its squat funnel started to move
down Southampton Water. White billowy clouds
hung in the blue sky; the sunshine danced on the
waters; a soft breeze blew from the south-east. A
perfect English autumn afternoon. All the best blue,
white and gold pageantry of our climate hung out, so
to speak, for the farewell. Lower down Southampton
Water we picked up another grimy black troopship,
festooned with heads and shoulders hanging over the
sides, and together slowly proceeded towards Spithead.
The nurses, stewards and attendants of a hospital ship
released round upon round of cheers as we passed.

" Bring him back alive," boomed a voice over the
waters during a pause.

England's last instruction to us! Nobody need be
told the name of the gentleman referred to. A vast
roar of cheering rose from both troopships.

Shortly after, anchor was dropped in Spithead, a

hundred yards from a couple more transports that were to cross to France in our convoy, and we settled down to wait for darkness, when the boom between the mainland and the Island would be opened for us to pass through and meet the destroyer escort outside.

The Colonel joined the Captain on the bridge. I, as you already know, had rendezvous at the ship's rail with the grey house over on the Island, and also with a big chunk of my past. The rest of the ship gave itself up to letter-writing unabashed. At every corner of the deck you saw them, officers and men, writing, writing, and very disagreeable if interrupted. These were really the last farewells—postscripts to the already spoken farewells—before England faded behind, perhaps for ever. Thus they were invested with a solemn importance which made itself felt. When the light of day waned the writing was still going on and men went below to finish their letters with the aid of dimmed lights behind closed portholes. Thousands and thousands of words must have been written in those few hours when we lay in Spithead before venturing into the Unknown. Thousands and thousands of echoes from the surcharged hearts of hundreds of brave men. I hope the Censor at Cherbourg dealt kindly with them.

For it was to Cherbourg we were going, though nobody on board knew it then. Midnight approached ; a black, moonless, starless night. Externally the ship was in utter darkness ; likewise the three other troopships lying a hundred yards away. Within the ship there was almost complete silence. The orgy of letter-writing had subsided, and now it was sleep's turn.

Midnight. The moment when the boom was to be opened in the centre by the Guardship and we were to emerge. On the stroke of twelve up ran our combination of red and white lights to indicate we were ready to move. Away outside the boom the Morse lamps on a destroyer twinkled back the signal : " Come along." We began to move slowly forward.

Suddenly, furious Morse signalling from the Guard-ship. Our boat gives a great shudder and stops, fully a quarter of a mile from the boom

The first mate of the troopship joins me in the bows.

" They've just signalled the boom is fouled," he says. " Can't open it. I'm not surprised. Two days ago a U-boat was sunk just outside. I expect the wreckage has fouled it."

There was nothing to do but drop anchor and wait.

2.30 a.m. Suddenly the Morse lights again begin to twinkle vigorously in the darkness. The boom is open at last. Cautiously we move forward through the gap in the centre. As we pass the Guardship, not more than twenty feet away, a voice from the bridge shouts our name.

" Ay, ay," comes the Guardship's response. We pass. And the boom is closed behind us.

The four troopships proceed, line ahead, to meet the destroyers. Everything is undisturbed blackness again. Our boat is last of the four and we follow the tiny red stern light of the ship ahead, little bigger than the glow of a cigarette-end. Over all is a silence that matches the darkness in its ponderosity, and its suggestion of looming, breath-bating mystery. And just when we are beginning to feel lonely we become aware that we have company. Two low, dark patches appear on each side of the line of troopships, coming from nowhere, like sudden crystallisations of the black night itself. They are the hulls of the destroyer escort to whom our destinies for several uncertain hours have been entrusted.

With the advent of the destroyers the troopships changed formation, henceforth moving two abreast. Our course is zig-zag, in longish narrow tacks. The destroyers manœuvred round us with astonishing

15

speed and agility. Suddenly they would tear out of the darkness, race alongside us, and disappear as dramatically, leaving only a pale wake to show their passing. They were behind us, in front of us, encircling us—everywhere, it seemed, at once, never letting go of us, combing every yard of the sea about us, a most comforting sight on this dark night of war.

From nowhere a destroyer shot out of the darkness right across our bows. It was gone in a flash. I think I must have gasped. I heard a low chuckle beside me. It was the affable first mate.

" Smart work isn't it ? " he said.

I agreed heartily.

" Bit too smart, almost, when the first convoys went over," he continued. " The skippers weren't used to it as they are now. One of 'em saw something suddenly bob up in front of him in the dark, like that destroyer just now. Thought it was a U-boat. Went for it to ram it. Of course, he missed. Still, you never know what might have happened."

From the first mate I learned that we were bound for Cherbourg. The captain had received his orders from the destroyers when we had cleared the boom.

" And we'll have a nice quiet trip, too," added the first mate. " This is the fastest convoy in existence. Average of twenty-two knots between the boom and port. That's good going. As for getting hit, well, it's nigh impossible unless the U-boat knew the course and was lying in wait. And that isn't very likely."

The first mate proved correct. It was a nice quiet trip. Three miles from Cherbourg, for the first time, our nose pointed straight towards our destination. Dawn was breaking as the low line of the French coast met our gaze. A French seaplane came out to meet us and swept round in circles till we reached Cherbourg Harbour, where the destroyers dropped behind to return to England.

And the little bit of England that was us set foot on French soil.

I'm afraid we all found it something in the nature of an anti-climax. Undoubtedly we had expected a welcome. We had expected cheers, and smiles, and perhaps kisses. We had read that such things happened to the first British soldiers to land in France in 1914. And we were not far behind the very first in 1939. We expected we would be going into battle almost immediately. We were sure the French would be overjoyed to see our faces and our new battle-dress.

Perhaps we were foolish to expect all this. Perhaps times have changed. Perhaps this is a war in which nobody feels inclined to cheer. Or perhaps we were just unlucky.

Still, the fact remains that when we landed at Cherbourg at 8 a.m. on a dreary and depressing morning the crowds assembled to welcome us consisted of a French naval sentry, some old market women, a fisherman or two and three gendarmes. As a reception committee they were a decided failure. They vouchsafed us a disinterested glance or two, and then went about their business.

And some of us had actually expected kisses !

II—" DESTINATION UNKNOWN "

" Wake up. The war's over," shouted the Major, at the same time ramming his heavy elbow into my ribs.

The ramshackle train gave a terrific jolt and expired. At first, shooting up from the ground floor of a slumber fathoms deep, I could easily imagine we were back in England again. Beyond the train windows it might have been the wooded rolling country of the Hampshire highlands that the morning sun was displaying in its early autumn tints.

Hour after hour from midnight we had rumbled down south-east from Cherbourg towards our " Destination Unknown." And here we were at last. Or so the regiment thought as it tumbled out on to the grass-grown railway track, in various stages of sleepiness and undress.

This was the Big Mystery, was it ? Half a dozen houses or so in one short street, a café and a streak of railway station labelled La Hutte. Now we knew.

But, as a matter of fact, we didn't. " Destination Unknown " was still in the blue. All that had happened was that we had broken the journey at La Hutte to await transport to convey us to " somewhere in France " where we were to pick up our guns.

So we piled equipment by the wayside, and set about making ourselves welcome. Otherwise I don't think the few inhabitants would have noticed us at all. Indeed, they betrayed a superb lack of curiosity. They didn't even think anything of us as freaks. As for genuine interest——

Still they were a long way from the Siegfried Line. They had been a long, long way from the last war. And it is very true of war that, even if distance does not lend enchantment to the view, it certainly does dull the sharpness of its outlines, and the force of its impact. We were to notice this later, as we drew closer to the line. There the civilian population did not disguise the fact that they regarded our presence, and that of the other British troops, as a matter of vital importance to them. We no longer wondered whether we were welcome. But in those first days in France we did miss not only a welcome, but even a show of ordinary interest. We thought it odd, when we thought about it at all. In our own defence, let it be remembered that we still believed we were going straight into battle.

The sentry lounging against his rifle at the level crossing just outside the station symbolised the in-difference of the village. A couple of cows grazing in an adjacent field occupied far more of his attention than the sudden descent of a regiment of British artillery. Of course, the cows might have belonged to him. In which case one can understand. He was a middle-aged reservist, wearing a tin hat and clad in the obsolete horizon-blue uniform. His other principal garment, his beard, was anything but obsolete. It had all the luxuriance of a ten-days unhampered growth, and there seemed any amount of life in it yet. The French Army does not regard a clean chin as a mark of soldierly smartness, and the poilu who shaves more than once in six days on active service runs the risk of being thought eccentric.

Along the roadside opposite the sentry some of our gunners began to give themselves a morning shave. He bore the ordeal without flinching. His face ex-pressed neither envy nor reproof. If it said anything it was : " Do as you please. I'm sticking to mine. I'm not likely to get a better issue."

It was approaching twelve when a fleet of R.A.S.C. lorries rolled down the village street. Now we were "getting warm" This was our transport to "Destination Unknown." In a few moments all the regiment knew the coveted secret—St. Remy de Plain, a village some fourteen kilometres away to the east.

The Babe, who was our youngest subaltern, went into ecstacies as we drove into St. Remy. He was only nineteen, and not long from Haileybury. He was crazy about the Russian Ballet, and had an alarming eye for the picturesque. This time we forgave him. It really was a charming village set in magnificent country. Pretty white plaster houses skirted the narrow cobbled street. Away behind was a delightful old church and the ruins of a castle.

" It's fifteenth century, if a day," gloated the Babe.

He was right, too, Later we discovered that the castle had been sacked and burned by the English in the days of Joan of Arc. We were the first English soldiery to set foot in St. Remy since our countrymen had come with fire and slaughter. Now we were visiting it with billeting money, by way of a change.

" The church is eleventh century," added the Babe judicially. And he was right again.

A Mairie with the Union Jack and the Tricolour draped over the door, and a blacksmith's shop, embellished the winding street ; and from the side of the hill where we stood we looked over a lovely valley to a forest on a distant ridge. In the rich afternoon sunshine the picture was one of warm abiding peace wherein our battledress, startlingly incongruous, seemed to have intruded by horrible mistake.

Still, here we were. But the guns were not. It was a bit of a surprise. We had confidently anticipated their arrival. The Second-in-Command, who had come over a week previously to arrange the billeting, broke the news. Nothing had been heard of them since they left England. Whereupon the Adjutant began to harass Corps Headquarters over the telephone for news. Corps Headquarters was situated in a large town many miles away. They politely refused to be harassed.

" Our guns hadn't arrived ? Oh well, they would. When ? Sometime. Where were they ? Nobody could exactly say."

Then to the final crucial question : " Had they got over safely ? " the reply : " Yes, it was believed they had been landed."

And with that we had to be content. It was believed the guns had escaped the attentions of the U-boats. It was believed they were somewhere in France. But nobody knew where ; and nobody could say when we might expect them.

However, as Corps Headquarters did not seem to be worrying unduly it would have been a mere impertinence for us to start. So the regiment settled down to its billeting, not knowing how long the stay in Remy would be.

*   *   *   *   *

And it was now that Y–Battery mess first betrayed those decided domestic ambitions that were henceforth to distinguish it so sharply from Z–Battery mess, its sister. Why this should have been is mysterious. Certainly it was not because we were loaded with married men, who might be presumed to have acquired a leaning towards the domestic comforts. Of the fourteen officers comprising Y–Battery mess, only four were married, and that was one less than in Z–Battery mess. Nor could we be considered as having reached the staid in years. Most of us were a bit over, or a bit under, twenty-five. On the face of it we looked a most unlikely lot to go in for domestication.

But the fact remains. Wherever Y–Battery mess settled it became house-proud with all the fervour of a newly-wed couple. It went in for home comforts which it devised with astonishing ingenuity. Y–Battery mess sat round its own fireside in the cold wet evenings when Z–Battery mess went off gallivanting. This is not to say we never had our lapses. But what was spasmodic with us, was inveterate habit with them. They were never at home.

Which all means, of course, that Y–Battery mess was a very happy crowd, and knew how to amuse itself. The Colonel, who was married, would often stroll in from Headquarters mess after dinner and spend the evening with us, quietly smoking his cigar, while " the family life " went on around him undisturbed.

Now, at Remy, we were about to institute our first mess on foreign soil, and being what it was Y–Battery felt the full and historic import of the occasion.

" There's an empty house standing back from the main street opposite the church," said the Billeting Major. " It'll make an ideal mess."

Six of us who were not engaged on other duties went along to inspect. Soon we were facing a two-storied house with shuttered windows, and wondering how anything in such a state of complete and utter dilapidation could still stand up. The plaster had dropped off the front in great flakes ; the paint had been blistered off the door and the window sashes. " Empty," the Major had called it. But it was worse than empty. It was ruinous. No one had lived there for years. Inside the dust rose at our footsteps, half-choking us. We walked into festoons of cobwebs that hung from the walls and ceilings. The rooms were utterly bare and smelt mouldy.

"Tops," the Troop-Commander of N-Troop, was the first to give utterance.

"Fine," he boomed.   "Or in the words of the Major —ideal.   The mess servants can sleep upstairs.   This big front room for the mess.   Look alive, everybody. Stokes and Rapley, you run round to Drage's and tell them to send the furniture at once—in a plain van."

Without hesitation the two subalterns disappeared on their quest.   The mess servants attacked the cobwebs and the dust.   A fire was lit in the rusty grate. Batmen produced empty bottles into which candles were stuck, there being no lighting.   Stokes returned in due course with a long table which he had borrowed after much persuasion from a very suspicious Curé. Rapley had not found Drage's either ; but he had induced an old woman to part with several planks of wood which, when placed on logs, gave us something to sit upon.

By six o'clock, when dusk fell, the place had undergone a transformation.   The mess servants and batmen had worked wonders.   The cobwebs had gone, the dust was invisible, a cheery log fire burned in the grate, and the candles in the bottles stuck on the chimney-piece and on the Curé's table illuminated the room with a soft friendly glow.

"Good.   But still a trifle bare," said the Major, inspecting.   "Must be those dirty white plaster walls."

So we each took a sector of them, got out our pencils, and began a little interior decoration.   The Major produced a very creditable representation of two sailing yachts, about to collide terrifically because his perspective was all wrong.   I wore away half a good pencil shading in the Gunner's badge.   The C.P.O. (Command Post Officer) drew a very big pot of very unknown flowers.   And the L-Troop leader perpetrated the equally big head of an equally unknown species of girl—supposed to be his wife. There was also a good deal of what might be called Surrealiste art . . .

We stood back to criticise the effect.

"Something still missing," said N-Troop Commander, meditatively. He brooded over the problem for a moment. "I've got it," he exclaimed. "The very thing. Just wait a minute."

He dashed off to his billet, and returned with a large double page torn from a magazine, showing in photogravure a pair of American chorus girls at the end of a strip-tease act.

"There you are. All that was wanted to give the place just that homely touch," said the Troop Commander proudly, pinning it up over the mantelpiece.

He stepped round to the other side of the table and regarded his effort with the air of a connoisseur.

"Fine," he said. "Or, in the words of the Major—not you, sir ; Major Wilson—ideal. And don't fail to note the striking paradox. The more unfurnished the ladies, the more it furnishes the room."

The door opened and there entered the Babe.

"What do you think of it, Babe ? " asked the Troop Commander with pride.

The Babe rested a bored glance on the mantelpiece.

"What's it supposed to be ? " he asked with a stupendous assumption of innocence.

"Hell ! Never mind what it's supposed to be," said the Troop Commander. "Doesn't it furnish the room ? "

The Babe seemed to take a few seconds for consideration.

"Candidly, no," he began loftily. "Now if it had been Tchernicheva in Petrushka, or . . ."

"Well, you asked my opinion," he said, when the laughter subsided.

We drifted off to our billets to tidy ourselves up for our first dinner in our first mess on foreign soil.

24

An hour later, on the way back, I met the N-Troop Commander and we went in together. The Major and all the other officers were gathered round the fire, and very comforting the room looked in the mellow candle-light, with the Curé's table laid for dinner, and the Dubonnet already in action.

The Troop Commander threw a beaming glance over the scene.

" Home, Sweet . . . "

He began but did not finish. Instead he stared speechless at the mantelpiece. The wall was bare. The unfurnished ladies who, " by a striking paradox, were to furnish the room and give it the homely touch," had vanished. By the side of the grate lay a ball of paper which told its own tale.

" Who's been playing the fool ? " demanded the Troop Commander crossly.

No one could enlighten him. None of the officers had so much as touched his masterpiece. Not even the Babe, who felt slightly under suspicion.

" A clear case for ' Oodunit ' proceedings, sir," said the Troop Commander.

The Major nodded.

So the mess servants were brought in one by one and questioned. One by one they exonerated themselves. Followed three or four of the batmen who had been sent along late in the afternoon to give the mess servants a hand. And among them Gunner McKinley.

Now Gunner McKinley hailed from Liverpool and was R.C.—which in the Army means Roman Catholic. He was a thin, alert, sandy-haired little fellow, getting on for forty, and with a watery blue eye.

" Did you pull that picture down ? " asked the Major.

" Yes, sir," replied McKinley firmly.

" Why ? "

25

"Well, sir, I didn't think it was the right sort of thing for the officers to see."

Staggering ! We thought there could never have been such an unexpected reply to any question ever asked. The Troop Commander flushed furiously. The rest of us struggled to keep from yelling with laughter. Only the Major remained impassive and continued his questions.

The extenuating circumstances proved to be that McKinley thought the picture had been pinned up by one of the mess servants.

The Major delivered judgment. " In future, McKinley, you will confine yourself strictly to the usual duties of batman. If and when I do think the officers' morals need attending to I'll let you know. Understand ? You can go."

He went. And just in time, for we were in much pain. Only the Troop Commander refused to see the funny side of it.

" Of all the damned cheek ! " he exclaimed.

While we enjoyed it he picked his treasure out of the grate and began to massage it carefully. But McKinley had done his job well. The creases defied the Troop Commander's expert touch. Finally, utterly disgusted, he pitched it into the fire.

" Now, if it had been Tchernicheva in Petrushka," began the Babe, blandly.

*   *   *   *   *

Spluttering like a Chinese cracker, a Don R (Despatch Rider) on a motor-cycle dashed up the steep village street bringing the big news. While nosing around the neighbourhood he had sighted the missing guns. They were twelve miles away, and would be here in half an hour.

Electrifying news. For three days the regiment had kicked its heels in Remy, completely ignorant of the whereabouts of the guns. The men were sick of marching drill, and the subalterns of shadow-ranging and revolver practice in the Castle moat. We all craved to be on the move. In those early days we feared the War wouldn't wait for us.

It was late in the afternoon. In a few seconds the sleepy village buzzed like a hive. Guides dashed off to meet the column and lead it to the gun-parks and vehicle-parks already selected. Out of billets and cafés poured sergeants, bombardiers and gunners in scores, eager to give the newcomers a healthy welcome.

Dusk was falling as the head of the column slowly rumbled into the village street with the weary-looking M-Troop Commander of Y-Battery in the leading tractor. A roar of cheers went up, and when it died away the fusillade of back-chat began. It was immense fun. Cockney chaff and pawky North-Country humour of the George Formby type predominated. Considering the drivers had driven more than a hundred and thirty miles that day over glaring roads, that they were worn-out, that they had sore eyes and dusty throats, their repartee must be reckoned first-class. Friend met friend as Greek is supposed to meet Greek in the proverb. A grand family reunion.

They kept it going, ripe and lusty, all the time the mile and a half column threaded into the village. Staff vehicles first, followed by the guns and ammunition trailers. The B-echelon vehicles brought up the rear. Very important, these, for they were the lorries containing the stores and the cooks' equipment. The good feeding of the regiment depended on them. Nor did the men forget it when they hove in sight.

Soon the guns were parked under hedges in a big field. The tired drivers were closely following a troop-sergeant to the cook-house. Y-Battery mess was proudly exhibiting its ideal home to M-Troop Commander and Harper and Thorpe, the two subalterns who

27

had accompanied him with the guns. It was their initiation to their first mess on foreign soil. Village champagne had been procured to grace the ceremony.

Admittedly, the vintage was not good. Admittedly, it suffered from other complaints. But that was no reason why Harper should have turned a sickly green the instant he put his lips to it.

" What's gone wrong with your face, Harper ? " I asked. " It looks ghastly."

Now, Harper, a Civil Servant when wars weren't being waged, possessed a dramatic turn of speech and a certain proficiency in the satirical.

" It's the Mark of the Beast," he replied in a hollow tone.

" Don't be rough on a champagne that's doing its best," protested Tops.

" He means the Bay of Biscay," explained M-Troop Commander, with a grin. " He'll tell you about it."

" Slow death for four unsolid days," began Harper, with intensity. " I've never liked Hitler. But if one of his U-boats had bobbed up and mercifully torpedoed me I'd have wrung his hand and called him friend and saviour."

" Very nice for you. But what about us, left with no guns," said the Drag Rope.

Harper turned on him a greenish smile.

" What about you ? Why, all the time my heart bled for you," he said gently. " Tears of pity filled my eyes at the thought of all you unfortunate fellows hanging about on hard dry land, with nothing to do but drink Dubonnet, while I was comfortably tucked up in my bunk on a free pleasure cruise. Sea-sickness takes you like that—if you don't happen to know. . . ."

He broke off and looked across at me.

" I want to hear you once more assure us that the War is going to last for years and years," he said.

" Why ? "

28

" So that I'll never have to cross the sea again."

Above the laughter rose the voice of M-Troop Commander addressing the Major.

" Any V.C.s going, sir ? I've had to put up with it ever since we landed."

*　　*　　*　　*　　*

Wafted down the street from the direction of the men's billets came the sound of familiar music.

Unlike the infantry, the artillery do not as a rule sing on the march. There isn't much point in letting it go when you are riding in a tractor. It doesn't make the wheels go round any the smoother. And there is such disheartening competition from other noise. But, like other regiments, we had our own weird and varied repertoire ; the difference being that while others sang on the move, the gunners and drivers sung when they were not, namely, in billets, at halts, and in the barn when the cinema broke down.

This evening they were celebrating the reunion with a regimental favourite based on the traditional Army theme—the Sergeant-Major.

" THEY (*with emphasis and pause*) . . . call it ' Bravery on
　　the field.'
　　THEY (*ditto*) . . . call it ' Bravery on the field.'
　　Our Sergeant-Major has got the D.C.M.
　　He got the D.C.M. for drinking all the rum ;
　　But when the shells come over
　　You should see the b—— run ;
　　THEY (*emphasis, no pause*) call it ' Bravery on the field.' "

The libellous libretto, pushed out with all the fervour of an anthem by scores of lusty, contented throats, ricochetted up and down the breezy street in the darkness.

Truly, the family were together again.

*　　*　　*　　*　　*

Oddly enough, it was the Colonel who had least reason to be completely satisfied with the day. He had got his beloved guns safe at last. All the vehicles, tractors and trailers had done the journey from England without mishap. But his own private car had not.

There was a shortage of dockers at St. Nazaire when the ship arrived, and the gunners had had to unload it themselves. As luck would have it, the one and only casualty was the Colonel's car. It took a fearful welt which completely buckled up the near-side door, jamming it so that it couldn't be opened.

The Colonel loved that 8-cylinder limousine. It was practically new. Very smart, apart from its camouflage.

He bore the blow well. I know, because I delivered the sad tidings. The chances of repair were negligible for some time.

A pity. But, as the Babe observed : " War is War."

III—A Bit of Billeting

Next Peace we have, I've made up my mind to be startlingly kind to any house-to-house canvasser who tries to sell me a vacuum-cleaner I don't want, or a three months' subscription to a newspaper I dislike. I shan't be thinking of his poor wife and child. I shall be thinking of his poor feet.

This good resolution seized me in the cobbled streets of Louviers after several hours intensive billeting. Never did I know stones were so brutal. Previously I thought stones were just stones. But they are much more depraved. My aching feet said so.

Heaven knows how many miles I had walked, north, south, east, west, round and round the town, and then round again, with a long list of billeting propositions in my hand, ticking them off as they met requirements. The modest boulevards, lined with chestnut trees, had looked attractive when I first arrived. But by now they represented so many yards of additional purgatory.

" How are your feet, George ? " I asked Anderton, the Captain from Z–Battery who was my fellow martyr.

" Haven't got any," he replied tersely.

The trouble was we had no time for rest. The regiment was moving forward. George and I had left Remy a day ahead of them to do the billeting. We had over seven hundred officers and men to bed down. That included the Light Aid Detachment (Royal Army Ordnance Corps) and the Royal Corps of Signals personnel attached to the regiment. No easy job, even taken at leisure. And we hadn't leisure.

Louviers was first stop, a hundred and forty miles north-east from Remy. George and I drove in early in the evening. At the Hotel de Ville I found a British Staff officer doing the billeting for the 2nd Division. Then it was plain what had happened. Having to wait for the guns had put the regiment behind schedule. It should have gone forward with the 1st Division. Now it was sandwiched between the 1st and 2nd Divisions.

However, the Staff officer gave us a list of addresses. It was too late to begin work on them. George and I billeted ourselves in a block of flats, while our drivers and batmen slept amid all the splendour of gorgeous chandeliers and red-plush furniture in the vast ball-room of the Hotel de Ville, having solemnly sworn to keep their dirty boots off the settees.

At daybreak we began. At midday I gave a sigh of relief.

"About finished, haven't we?" I said, hopefully.

"Another hundred to place," reported George, gloomily, checking the list.

That meant we had to go all over the ground again to squeeze the hundred in. Roughly, you billet by paces. One man to a pace. Thus, suppose a room is twelve feet wide and fifty paces long, then you billet a hundred men there—fifty along each side. We'd have given a lot for just such a room now.

Up and down the cobbled streets for another hour and a half. More pacing and re-pacing. More mental arithmetic.

At last I ventured to look hopefully at George again. He checked the list.

"All brought to bed," he announced at last. " Whew! That's the biggest hundred ever. Now for

the Mouton d'Or. If I don't have some food my feet
will faint."

But I had one thing more to do. I had billeted the
Colonel on a wealthy mill-owner, a big, hearty Norman,
who had a beautiful house by the side of the canal.

I hobbled over to have one last word with him.

" You asked me, monsieur, what special thing you
could do to please the Colonel. I've just thought of
it. Give him three grilled rashers of bacon and a
couple of eggs for breakfast. He hasn't tasted any
since he left England."

" Yes, yes. That is good. I will," he said, with a
big laugh.

Duty done, I rejoined George at the Mouton d'Or.

It should have been a hurried meal because we had
to push on to Abbeville, another hundred miles or so,
before evening. But the cognac was good, and our
feet were bad, and just as we did think of shifting, in
walked the Captain of another artillery regiment who
had just turned up to do his bit of billeting.

So we stayed on longer to hear the story of how
he had ingeniously smuggled his shooting brake across
from England disguised as a regimental truck, all
camouflaged in regulation style, and painted with the
regimental tactical sign. He was very proud of the
feat, and we enjoyed the gleeful description of how
he had lured the transport officer at the port of
embarkation into conversation, so that he had mis-
counted the number of vessels loaded. He promised
himself much useful reward for his trouble. He had
a prevision that sooner or later the authorities would
frown on the use of army trucks by officers for
excursions that were not strictly military. I congratulated him on his foresight, and began to toy
with the idea of Y–Battery mess clubbing together
to buy a communal Citroen, in case the worst happened.

And so meditating, and looking out of the window

to see what the new hubbub in the boulevard was about, I beheld with astonishment Y–Battery Commander's truck rolling up the street. There could be no doubt. There was the familiar regimental sign superimposed on the G.H.Q. red, white and blue square on the mudguard, and the tactical sign X (Major) on the plate in front.

The regiment, moving fast to make up for lost time, had caught us up.

I dashed out, had a brief word or two with the Colonel, showed him his bacon-and-egg billet, and in a few minutes was speeding after George in my truck on the road to Abbeville.

It was pretty late when we drove in. This time we were ahead of any British Staff officer. No one was expecting the arrival of the regiment. I went across to the French cavalry barracks and interviewed the Commandant. No. He was unaware that any British were due. I explained that I understood that our regiment was to be billeted in some village just outside Abbeville. Had he received any information ?

No ; none at all. However, he had the idea it would be Doudainville, a village about five miles outside the town. He gave me a demand note on the Mayor. And with that I had to be content.

*   *   *   *   *

Early next morning we went in search of Doudainville. We were now in the district of the Lower Somme—flat, bare country, unadorned by trees, and all cut up by canals and big ditches with dreary grey osier willows growing along the banks. It was damp and chilly, and a thick ground mist hovered over the fields. The sky was grey, and spitting rain.

Doudainville, when we found it, fitted very well into this dismal scene. It was a fairish-sized village, but half the houses were in ruins and deserted. The

Mayor was away at a distant village, so his deputy, an aged farmer, showed us round.

The survey was not promising. Billeting at Louviers was going to be a picnic compared with this. There our feet got hurt. Here our brains were going to suffer. How to decently bed over seven hundred men in the scanty and ruinous accommodation offered by Doudainville would be a hard sum.

Added to which, I wasn't even sure that Doudainville was the right village. Still, it was necessary to take a chance about that. No use hanging about Abbeville waiting for instructions to arrive. More likely the regiment would arrive first, at the pace they were travelling. Better bad billets at Doudainville than none at all.

So deciding, George and I began our investigation of half-roofed barns, tumbledown outhouses, and dilapidated farm buildings, with an odd cottage and house thrown in. Hour after hour we measured and counted, condemned and approved. We had a gunner on a motor-cycle with us, and half-way through I sent him down the road towards Louviers to act as a guide for the regiment.

Then happened one of those little incidents that, when they occur (and they occurred fairly frequently to the B.E.F.) give one the sensation of having raised a ghost. On the edge of the village stood a small farmhouse in a very ruinous condition. It was utterly deserted, and obviously hadn't been tenanted for years. I opened the door which led straight into a room. Chalked in big letters on the opposite wall was the command :

WIPE YOUR FEET, PLEASE.
1918.

It was so peremptory that I almost obeyed, forgetting that this was not 1918 but 1939, and that only the

35

ghosts of a past officers' mess in a past war would
grouse if I didn't.

For that was what the place had been—some
infantry mess. And it stood there exactly as it had
been left after the Armistice. I could almost imagine
that, with terrible clairvoyance, its occupants had
foreseen that it might be wanted again. In a corner
was a rusty bayonet and a Mills bomb. The stained
deal table and the three wooden chairs were thick
with the dust of twenty-one years of peace. In a
little cupboard were the remains of a bottle of tomato
ketchup, a tin of Nestle's milk, some empty tins of
sardines and four half-empty bottles of wine. There
was something pathetic about this little heap of
forlorn-looking debris, a legacy from one British army
to another, black and mouldy, but a reminder of
many things.

I left the place as I found it. There are more
unlikely things than that the man who chalked that
exhortation on the wall in 1918 may have read it
again.

The billeting progressed laboriously, but definitely
towards a conclusion. It was raining pretty hard
now. Nevertheless, George and I were beginning to
feel happy. We were priding ourselves on a tough
job well accomplished.

Suddenly, round the corner of the street came the
Colonel in his car. He had come ahead of the
regiment to find us, and had picked up our guide on
the road. He brought information.

" Clear out of here," he said. " You're in the
wrong village. It's Moulainville."

I couldn't bear to look at George. To think we'd
got to go through the same racket twice in one day.
I looked at the big dent in the Colonel's car. And I
was sure that somewhere inside me was a dent just
about as big.

So we boarded our trucks again and set off for Moulainville, which was five miles away. The Colonel accompanied us, and when we arrived billeted himself at the Mairie. So that was off our conscience.

Now, I don't know whose wise thought it was that the regiment should be billeted at Moulainville. Whoever it was, he'd have done far better to have thought of Doudainville, poor as it was. When George and I began to explore Moulainville we felt so horrified that we had to pay a visit to the mayor for something to revive us. The Mayor, long-moustached and as lugubrious as his village, produced two bottles of ten-year-old cider, which behaved very well. His wife fortified us with slices cut from a huge farm-house cake.

Munching away, my mind was revolving round the problem of Moulainville and its reconciliation to the ethics of billeting. For there are certain ethics to be observed in billeting on the march. You discover them quickly if you want to lead a happy life.

One is that the Colonel must always be billeted in the most important-looking house in the town or village. Not the most comfortable, mark you—the most important. For instance, if you allot him a nice clean, picturesque, comfortable little cottage— the sort of place he'd buy on sight if he saw it at home —when there is an ugly, half-tenanted, dusty-roomed Mairie a little further up the street, you lose marks.

Secondly, it is wisdom to do your Battery Commander proud, within your limits.

Thirdly, look after yourself. Because no one else will. Besides, you will be accused of having done so in any case.

As to other officers, you do your best by them ; and if they don't like it, you don't worry. You can be sure they won't like it, whatever you do. It helps, sometimes, when they arrive to take them aside separately, and tell each what a superb billet you've found him—*before he sees it*!

There's always an outside chance he may prefer your enthusiasm to the evidence of his own eyes.

But as I sat munching the mayoress's cake, I had to admit that I couldn't raise a fraction of the enthusiasm required to blind anyone's eyes to the true facts about the billets at Moulainville.

The Colonel had tucked himself in. That was one consolation. Another was that we were all in the same boat. Every billet was going to be as bad as every other one. There would be room for grumbling, but none for odious comparison.

And so it worked out.

IV—Nemesis Stalks Abroad

It was at Moulainville that Nemesis stalked abroad.

I've never liked Nemesis. I liked her even less when I found that, with all the deserving cases in the regiment, she must needs go and drop the heavy dirty paw of Retribution on Driver Timms.

Driver Timms was my personal driver. He was a possession in which one could take legitimate joy and pride. By far he was the best driver in the Battery, if not in the regiment. Later on, when Driver Timms' affairs reached the stage of discussion in Y-Battery mess, Tops, N-Troop commander, championed him without reserve.

" There's no driver I'd sooner go into action with, sir," he told the Major. " That fellow would drive through the hottest barrage."

Yes, there was no doubt he had daring. And he was smart, too. Smart on parade, smart in finding his way about, smart in his battle-dress, which is saying something.

Unhappily, it was his smartness that drew Nemesis towards him as irresistibly as the magnetic mine is drawn to the liner.

Coming out of the mess the evening the regiment billeted down at Moulainville, I walked across to the village square where I had parked my truck, containing all my kit, in charge of Driver Timms, and my batman, Williams. I had been pretty hard at work for fourteen hours, and thought it was about time I prepared my own billet. So I wasn't too pleased when I found that truck driver and batman had

39

completely disappeared.   I sent search parties out and
waited hopefully.   They found nothing, not even a
clue.   I was left with just the clothes I was standing
in.   Bed, bedding, everything gone.

I couldn't imagine what had happened.   I'd given
both the men orders to wait on the square till I returned.   Hours went by and no sign of them.   Finally
I had to share the bed of another officer.

Apart from other considerations, I was a bit upset
about losing the truck.   There was sure to be a row
about that.   All C.O.s hate to lose a truck.   These
useful little vehicles are quite a feature of the mechanised army.   They seat four, with the driver, the two
rear seats being for the wireless operators.   They are
canvas-roofed, with flaps but no windows, and the
aerial which sticks up on top is detachable.   You
detach it, of course, when you are using the truck—
well, to do your shopping in.   Big low pressure balloon
tyres, two-ton weight, 24 h.p. Morris engines.   They
do forty miles per hour, and can do eighty if you take
the governor off.   That, by the way, is a crime.   The
front of the truck is adorned with the red, white and
blue G.H.Q. sign, on which is superimposed the regimental number, and a yellow disc on which the weight
appears in black.   This is for the use of sentries
at bridges.   In front of the radiator is a plate carrying
what is known as the tactical sign which designates
the occupant of the truck, thus K (Captain), X (Major),
Z (Colonel), and so on.

Not inconspicuous little objects by any means ; yet
it was astonishing what curious things could happen
to trucks.   The talk was that the First Corps alone
had lost a hundred in a week.

So I could feel a very cold eye awaiting me
next morning when I had to report another had
gone.

At 1 a.m. I was wakened by my bedfellow.

" Hyde's outside, yelling for you," he said, and
went to sleep again.

Outside the window was the G.P.O. (Gun Position
Officer) of M-Troop. Two men had come in and
reported that my truck was stranded in Abbeville.

" What about the driver ? "

" He's been taken to hospital with appendicitis."

" And Williams is holding his hand. Thanks,
Hyde," I said. " Send a truck and a spare driver
over to bring mine back. And tell them to find out
whether Timms is really in hospital. And tell them
to bring Williams back."

I went back to my half-share of bed with, at any
rate, two-ton weight of truck off my mind.

Next morning, before the Major, we heard, via
Williams, how Nemesis works. Not expecting I should
leave the mess so soon, Timms had proposed a little
dash into Abbeville, five miles away, a dance or two
at a dance-hall, and back again without questions
being asked. It would have worked all right if Timms
hadn't fallen to the ground in agony the instant he
alighted from the truck at Abbeville. He was taken
to hospital with acute appendicitis. Williams, who
couldn't drive himself, had a lonely and apprehensive
vigil till the rescue party arrived.

The regiment had left Moulainville a month before
Timms rejoined us, pale and thin after his operation,
but as smart as ever. The Major had him up, pointed
out the seriousness of the offence, gave him some
good fatherly advice, and ended by saying that
as Nemesis, in the shape of the surgeon's knife, had
forestalled him, he wouldn't punish the culprit any
more.

This was satisfactory to me, as I wanted to get my
jewel of a driver back again. I hoped Nemesis had
finished with him. But she hadn't.

I came down to the Battery Office one morning

about six weeks later, and waiting for me was a very worried-looking Timms.

" K truck (mine) has been stolen," he announced dolefully.

Now this was getting serious. I began to feel that Nemesis was after me, too. I reported the theft to the Major, who reported it to Regimental Head-quarters, and then, with the help of the Battery Sergeant-Major, we began to cross-examine Timms. He stuck to his story. He had filled up at 4 p.m. the previous afternoon and parked the truck in the usual place behind the Battery Office, and in the morning it was gone. He doubted our united ability to conceive what a surprise it had been to him.

The Battery Sergeant-Major cocked a cynical eye at him.

" And where were you last night ? " he asked.

" I spent the evening in a café in the village with Gunner Simmonds."

We all felt there was something odd about it. But we had nothing definite to go on. As I left the Battery Office with the B.S.M. he exploded :

" I'll get to the bottom of this, sir, even if it takes me the whole war."

When I saw the Sherlock Holmes' glint in his eye I hoped Timms's alibi was right, for his own sake.

The B.S.M. spent a day and a half snooping round, picking up odd bits of conversation and keeping his eyes open. After a time he noticed a truck belonging to another regiment parked in the village square. It stood there all day long. It was there in the evening with no lights turned on. The B.S.M. grew suspicious. He ordered a driver to take the truck down to the guard, and had a man put on it. Then, with a new idea in his mind, he confronted Timms.

The B.S.M. had guessed right. Timms confessed that he had taken my truck into Douai on the fatal night, parked it in the Grand Place, and gone to a dance-hall. When he came out the truck was gone, so, panic-stricken, he helped himself to one belonging to another regiment.

This time there was no appendicitis to save him. He was for it. He was court-martialled by the Colonel. I lost my treasure of a driver. I was sorry to part with him. He was really a smart fellow. Only Nemesis was smarter.

V—In The Line

The Colonel stood beside his car at the end of the
winding road leading into Auchy.   Before him rolled
the long column of rumbling tractors, guns, trailers
and other vehicles.   It was late in the afternoon.   A
cloudy, sunless day.   But the gloom did not conceal
the Colonel's satisfaction.   Every driver, every gunner
as the regiment passed under his eye knew that the
" old man " was pleased.

He had every reason to be.   The regiment had now
reached its destination.   It had covered some four
hundred miles in three days, without a single casualty
or a single man falling sick.   Not a bad record for
over seven hundred men, all of whom, a week or so
before, had been civilians sleeping in comfortable beds
at night.

As for the speed with which we had moved, that
was a triumph for mechanisation.   We still had a few
recalcitrants in the regiment who pinned their faith
to horses, and never looked at a tractor without a
shudder.   Though it was several years since we said
good-bye to our horses, they hadn't become reconciled
to the change.   They prophesied gloomily, and sneaked
round when nobody was looking to take a sentimental
peep at the old regimental trumpets which the Quartermaster had brought over in his store, for old times'
sake.

But four hundred miles in three days.   They couldn't
answer that.

We were now in the line.   Half a mile or so in front
was the infantry of the Division, spread out over a

broad front.   More were pouring in from behind us.
We still expected that the storm would burst at any
moment.   Had anyone told us then that we should
remain at Auchy for nearly three months without firing
a round (barring the ack-acks), we should have laughed.

Also we should have been disappointed.   There was
no doubt about the fighting spirit of the regiment.
They had left their homes in England to do a nasty
job, and the sooner the better.   Not a gunner, not a
driver, but was well on his toes.   The sergeants knew
it, the Troop Commanders knew it, the Battery Commanders knew it, and the Colonel knew it.   Hence his
pride.   Moreover, he had fought with the regiment
through the last war.   So he had a fatherly attitude
towards it, too, which the men appreciated.   He knew
he could rely on them, and they knew they could rely
on him.

As I have said, we were all civilians, who had learned
to handle guns in evenings after work and holidays.
There was a sprinkling of officers and men who had
served in 1914–1918, but for the majority of us it was
our first war.   We were the new generation, you might
say.   The Colonel himself was only forty-five.   Every
trade and profession was represented, from stock-
brokers and lawyers to dock labourers and plate-
layers.   In truth, we were democratic enough for
anybody's taste.

Corps Headquarters were in touch with us as soon
as we put our noses into Auchy.   Down came a
Brigadier to show the Colonel over the regimental
area.   Then the Colonel escorted the Battery Commanders over the ground and Troop positions were
picked (four guns to a Troop).   These were approved
by the Colonel.   Back came the Brigadier to see them.

" Let me have a look at the map.   No, you can't
have that.   The —th are coming in round there.   You
can't have that either."

45

" That " and " that " were little reserved positions in the main area for troops coming up behind us. So our gun positions had to be revised.

At last it was settled. The gun-pits were dug, eighteen inches deep, and sandbagged five feet high in front. The circular steel gun platforms were hoisted off the trailers and embedded in the earth. The guns themselves are mounted on these with the wheels on the outer rim, so that they can be easily slewed round. Revetted trenches were constructed at the sides in case the enemy bombardment became very heavy.

It was hard work and had to be done quickly. As I have said, we expected to find ourselves in action any day. The gunners worked magnificently. Nothing could damp their spirits. Not even the soaking rain, which now began to pour steadily. It was to rain without ceasing for weeks, but, mercifully, that knowledge was hidden from us. The time was soon to come when our regimental area became a quagmire. Gun-pits were flooded, and instead of gunners we became drainage engineers. At every step you sank into mud a foot thick. Rain washed out billets. Dry clothes became a luxury. Useless the 1914–1918 veterans comforting us with the assurance that it couldn't be compared to the Flanders mud. It was good enough for us.

And just about this time letters began to arrive from home informing us what a nice time we were having.

When, after tremendous exertions at top-speed, our gun-pits were nearly finished along came a General to inspect. His verdict was that we " didn't seem to have done much." Next day another General appeared, and he assured us that General No. 1 " didn't know what he was talking about." So we **were happy** again. It could go on raining.

Our gun positions were in the neighbourhood of Nomains, about two miles from Auchy. Part of the regiment was billeted at Auchy, and a hundred men at Moncheaux about six miles away, where we had our Wagon Lines. Here, parked in and around the out-buildings of a farmhouse, were the tractors for the guns, and the two-ton and three-ton lorries for the gun stores, the Quartermaster's stores, the trailers with racks for ammunition, the officers' vehicle with the mess equipment, and the cook's vehicle which carried the men's mess apparatus. It was here that all our reserve ammunition was stored—about seventeen tons of shells and charges.

*   *   *   *   *

On the day the guns were to go into the pits the Colonel took a tour round. He had conceived the idea that in view of possible eventualities it would be a good thing to have the men billeted as near the guns as possible. There was nothing wrong with this.

Now N–Troop guns were just behind the hedge in a big ploughed field without any habitation in sight. But half a mile down the bend of the road was the municipal slaughter-house, with some unoccupied stables just behind.

"They might do," he said to me, with a casual glance at them as he drove off.

It was just a vague thought of his, and I was the only person to whom he communicated it. He said nothing more about it ; neither did I.

And now, mark the uncanny news-gathering instinct of the army. I was leaving the Mess after tea that afternoon when three sergeants of N–Troop approached with all the solemn air of a deputation.

"May we have a word with you, sir ? "

"Yes, what is it ? "

47

" We hear that we might be billeted in the slaughter-house."

" Well ? "

" We'd rather not, sir. Although there's no slaughtering at the moment, the very name affects us disagreeably."

Their pained expressions were really comical.

" Think no more about it," I said.

" Thank you, sir. We were sure you would understand."

I understood all right. And so did the Colonel when I mentioned it to him. But what we could not understand was how the merest flicker of an idea had travelled to them. It must be a sergeant's secret.

*   *   *   *   *

Still, N–Troop's position was henceforth nicknamed " The Slaughterhouse." By an odd coincidence the next position was known as " The Cemetery." Here the guns were under an embankment on which stood a cemetery, and were overlooked by tall white marble statues of the Virgin Mary, angels with hands folded over their bosoms, and bowed sorrowful heads, and great crosses. Very melancholy it looked in the twilight, if you happened to be superstitious. Next in order came " Paradise," so-called from the name of a farmhouse close by.

" The Slaughterhouse "—" Cemetery "—" Paradise." That was the order. Pessimists took a gloomy view of the progression. The optimists pointed out that you couldn't do better than Paradise, even if you stayed at home and died in your bed.

Anyhow, we were proud of " Paradise." It became a show place. Corps Headquarters sent the newspaper correspondents and the news-reel men along to do their stuff here. The gun-pits were models of what gun-pits should be. The sandbagging and revetting

48

were perfection. The drainage devices worked perfectly, and all the drainage channels were nicely boarded-in. It must have looked quite swagger on the films.

Most of the credit for this was due to the G.P.O. (Gun Position Officer) of L–Troop. He was a graduate of Magdalen College, Oxford, a fine classical scholar, and in civil life a solicitor. But as soon as the rain had lasted three days, he blossomed forth in the full flower of his real genius—drainage. Most of us thought it a marvel.

" Nothing of the sort," said N–Troop Commander. " He's a solicitor and used to getting blood out of a stone. Getting water out of a gun-pit is child's play to him."

The G.P.O. laughed, and said the Troop Commander was quite right.

VI.—A CONTRAST IN STYLES

It was just before dinner in Y–Battery Mess, and we were warming up to it with gin and vermouth after a very damp day. The principal noise was a lot of hefty German voices lifting the roof off with a Students' song. It came from Amherst's gramophone. Amherst was the Command Post Officer. He liked music, symphony-size preferred. Apart from this he had a fondness for German Student Songs. He was careful not to put the records on when we had French guests, military or civilian, to dinner.

In the middle of a rousing Teutonic fortissimo the door opened and a French officer appeared. The guttural welcome seemed to stagger him. Then Amherst turned the thing off, and the Frenchman recovered his balance.

Being senior officer present I went forward to greet him. He introduced himself as Pierre Mounier, our new Marechal de Logis, otherwise Liaison Officer. He was a fine, tall, broad fellow, with dark hair and a stiff clipped moustache. He made an imposing figure with the two rows of ribbons on his breast, including the ribbon of the personal Croix de Guerre, and the green and red tassel of the Croix de Guerre.

I accepted his statement with reserve. The overwhelming display of decorations may have influenced me. They looked too good to be true. But I knew we were expecting a Liaison Officer, so I ordered him a drink and hopped over to Headquarters Mess and brought back the Adjutant.

" Your credentials, monsieur, if you please," said the Adjutant.

They proved to be all right.

" You'd better have him to dinner. We haven't enough food," the Adjutant said to me.

And that was how Y–Battery Mess gained a new acquisition.

Acquisition he was. Pierre proved himself to be a man of many parts. To begin with he was a connoisseur of food and drink. He transformed the Mess. We made him the secretary, a thankless job, to be sure.. But he was delighted. Henceforth we dined *de luxe* off dishes fit for a Parisian restaurant. As a raconteur he was superb, and whether or not he knew all the people he said he did, the stories he told about them were funny enough. He was brave as a lion. He had served with distinction in the last war, and had travelled half across the world to be in this one. Though well into middle-age his one great desire was to get as near the fighting line as possible.

The thing that amused us most about him was not his stories but his excitability. Just as the thing that pained him most about us, and the British generally, was our phlegm as he called it. He could never understand why we took little mishaps, and occasionally big ones, so coolly. And we could never make him understand that volubility and gesticulation made no impression on the British soldier.

I had a billet on the second floor of a neat little white farmhouse in the main street of the village. One night, about three weeks after Mounier's arrival, I was awakened by hearing my name called from the street below, and called again, three or four times in great urgency. Looking at my watch I saw it was half-past one in the morning.

Not very pleased at being dragged out of bed I opened the window.

51

" Yes. What's the matter ? "

Pierre Mounier's agitated voice answered me.

" Come quickly. One of your troops has nearly murdered a taxi-driver."

Knowing the Liaison Officer's gift for exaggeration, I simply replied :

" It's half-past one."

" But he is bleeding to death," shouted Pierre frantically.

" Are you quite sure ? Remember, it is half-past one," I said coldly.

" It is urgent," he cried.

I put on my boots, greatcoat and cap, went down-stairs, and opened the front door. There was a little group outside, and the Liaison Officer detached him-self and stepped forward. He was a wonderful sight. He wore his peaked cap, and his tunic over a pair of short white pants. His feet were in bedroom slippers. In his hand he gripped a big Browning automatic.

" It's loaded," he said, to give me confidence, I suppose.

" I don't see any dying man," I remarked, looking around.

The Liaison Officer seemed to be taken aback.

" But he's standing next to you," he said.

I turned and saw a man bleeding from a small cut over the left eye. He treated me to an impassioned description of the row, with a vigour of illustration that was astonishing for a " nearly murdered " man.

" All right," I said to the Liaison Officer, yawning. " Get all the particulars, and take the man over to the M.O. to have his cut plastered. We'll go into it in the morning."

" But something must be done at once," said Pierre, excitedly.

" What do you propose ? "

He proposed that the whole regiment should be

52

instantly turned out of bed, and that all the men should have their knuckles inspected for abrasions.

" My dear Pierre," I said. " It is half-past one in the morning, and I'm going back to bed."

I left him still clinging to his automatic, and looking completely nonplussed by this latest example of British phlegm.

Next morning I reported the affair to Regimental Headquarters, and the details were forwarded to the British Military Police. But the Liaison Officer went about for days grieving that I had not paraded the regiment at half-past one on a cold morning.

Meeting him in the Mess one afternoon a few weeks later, I said :

" They've found the man who beat up your taxi-driver."

" Good ! But it is a long while. Now, if you had——" he began.

" It was a man from a neighbouring regiment," I interrupted with a grin.

VII—Air Reconnaissance

Pom-pom-pom-pom-pom . . .

Pom-pom-pom-pom-pom . . .

Pom-pom-pom-pom-pom . . .

The Bofors anti-aircraft guns suddenly began strumming at the rate of about fifty shells a minute. Bofors shells are fed to the gun five in a clip, like rifle cartridges. Hence their distinctive rhythm. Five insistent poms to the bar.

It was a fine sunny morning and the Major and I were alone in the Battery Office. The Major glanced at his new watch.

" Eleven-fifteen. This watch keeps fine time," he remarked with satisfaction.

The telephone bell rang. I picked it up.

" Air-Raid-Warning-Red," murmured a gentle, deliberate voice.

" Got it," I shouted back, and slammed down the receiver.

Headquarters. Giving us information we knew. We rarely got their warning until after the guns had opened fire. Outside a couple of bombardiers were already blowing whistles in short blasts. The men had adjusted their respirators to the " alert." The gas sentries were standing-to.

Not that we expected anything much to happen. These morning calls had become a bore. From the day the Division first came into the line the Germans had displayed an ardent curiosity regarding the British positions. Barely a morning passed without a couple of their reconnaissance planes showing up

And very punctually, too. Eleven-fifteen. That was why the Major could test out his new watch by their arrival.

I strolled out of the Battery Office to have a look, in case there did happen to be a dog-fight. But except for two specks disappearing down the line with the white plumes of the bursting Bofors shells around them, the blue sky was clear.

On this particular morning I felt some personal interest in those two planes. I could imagine their cameras softly whirring all the time, and wondered what the result would be. For a few hours later I was to do an air reconnaissance myself over much the same course, and with the specific object of seeing whether the camouflage of our battery positions was satisfactory from above. What should I see ? And what had their cameras seen ?

Corps orders were that I should fly over the gun positions and O.P. (Observation Posts) area, and traverse the Belgian frontier and mark down likely gun positions and approaches that the enemy might take if they came through that way.

At 2 p.m. I started off in my truck for the aerodrome. I had been given its map reference, and a forty-mile journey ended just south of Douai. Over on the airfield a Lysander army co-operation plane was busily ticking away, ready for me. The army liaison officer attached to the squadron took me across and introduced me to the pilot. He was a chubby, merry-eyed youth, and we went into a huddle over a map while I explained what I wanted to see, and also that I wished to fly down the line.

" Right," he snapped. " Come on. Can you fire a Vickers ? Because we may want to."

" Yes," I replied though I'd never done so in a plane.

" Good."

55

And I knew from his tone that on the slightest provocation we should see some fun. He was spoiling for a fight.

" Now this is important," he said, pointing to the loaded Very light pistol poked up through the top of the fuselage with the trigger inside. " Be sure to fire that at once if we are shelled by our own guns. They sometimes make mistakes. Those ack-ack gunners are so damned touchy."

I nodded. I knew all the stories.

" The other day," he went on, " a French pilot attracted their attention. All the English he could say when he got down was : ' What the hell ! What the hell ! ' Couldn't have done better if he'd known the whole blooming language."

He laughed cheerfully.

Meanwhile, the sergeant-aircraftman had been buckling on my parachute harness. He gave me a few hasty instructions in case I had to " jump for it." I hoped I should remember them. I climbed into the cockpit and clipped the parachute to the harness.

The pilot and I sat back to back, so I looked out over the tail of the machine, with the Vickers gun in front of me and pans of ammunition ready stacked on each side. " Thumbs up " was the signal I was ready, and off we went.

We climbed swiftly to four thousand feet. It was a fine afternoon, with visibility perfect. I was aware we had had some wet in our sector, but I was not prepared for the scene beneath me. The whole country-side appeared to be in the throes of an inundation. Acres and acres, fields and roads, were completely submerged. The trees jutted up from inland seas. Where the land was visible it merely resembled a network of causeways, linking together a lot of great lakes. It was pretty obvious there could be no mechanised warfare hereabouts for some time.

I turned my attention to the battery positions. Knowing where to look for them made it easier, of course, for me to spot them. But I saw things that would make it easy for other people. The quagmire into which our regimental area had been transformed by the continual rains revealed certain definite markings. They were the mud-tracks made by the gunners going to and from the gun-pits. I could guess how they would show on a camera film. Thin veins suddenly stopped by a small pimple. And the Germans would know those pimples were the gun positions. Perhaps they were already looking for them on the photographs taken by their planes that morning. Not a very comforting reflection. We flew over our show position, " Paradise." Out of twelve gun-pits only two were invisible. Certainly the weather had made havoc of our camouflage.

The plane rose another thousand feet, and we headed for the Belgian frontier. Soon we were humming along just this side of the long wide ditch that had been dug for mile after mile as a tank trap. Every two miles or so a huge white horizontal capital " B " marked the Belgian side of the frontier. Historic battle-grounds met my eye as we travelled southwards, opposite Ypres, Menin, Tournai and Mons. Battle-grounds where the regiment had won distinction over twenty years before. I wondered where our fate lay, and what it would be, this time.

We were taking a sweep round to the forts at Maubeuge when a speck appeared in the distant sky. Immediately the pilot began to climb, keeping his eye on it all the time. I started to pay attention to the Vickers. But in a moment or two he motioned to me that it was one of our planes. The shrug of his shoulders was truly expressive.

I got back to the mess in time for tea, after a very pleasant afternoon. When my report went in to the Brigadier he said he was not surprised I had seen what I had seen. He toyed for a while with the idea of constructing scores of dummy gunpits.

The entire regiment was grateful that he only toyed with it.

VIII—First Bloodshed

" The Colonel says that some of N–Troop billets are untidy. He was snooping round this morning," said the Major.

" I'll attend to it, sir," said the Troop Commander.

" What else . . . er . . . oh, yes. There are too many men reporting sick. I know the weather's bad. But see what's wrong," added the Major.

" Very well, sir," I replied.

The daily Battery conference was just concluding. It took place after tea, when the Major returned from the Regimental conference. He passed on to us the orders—and the kicks—as they affected Y–Battery. It was also the convenient time for discussing what may be called the domestic concerns of the Battery.

" One more thing," said the Major. " Christmas is coming. What about the men's dinner ? We can't hope the Government will supply us with turkeys."

Somebody suggested we should provide chickens.

" No good," said N–Troop Commander. " We should want hundreds. They're such skinny little devils round here."

" I thought pork," said the Major.

" Great thought, sir," exclaimed N-Troop Commander. " Roast pork with crackling. We'll buy two pigs and fatten them ourselves. It's just seven weeks to Christmas. They'll be juicy by then."

It was decided that Pierre Mounier should be entrusted with the task of scouting round the neighbourhood to find a farmer who had two pigs to sell.

59

" Who's going to look after them ? " asked the Major.   " Any pig experts in the Battery ? "

Gunner White was discovered in L–Troop who had actually been a pig-breeder. So he was made O.C. pigs and detailed off to go round the country-side with the Liaison Officer till he got a couple of healthy ones at the right price.

It took two weeks' search before they settled with a farmer for a pair at twelve hundred francs.   Meanwhile, a swagger sty had been constructed in a field down at the wagon lines.   On the great day a regimental truck was sent to collect the pigs, and for the first time in the War the camouflage net came in handy.   It proved the ideal contraption for keeping them in.

Pretty well all the regiment turned up at the wagon lines at midday to greet the arrivals.   The men cheered, the pigs squealed.   They were a fine-looking pair, already weighty, and full of life.   So much so, indeed, that there was decided hesitation on the part of the troops to enter the truck to get them out.   When volunteers were called for each man pushed someone else forward.   Our brave Allies came to our assistance in the shape of Mme. Mercier from the nearby farmhouse.   Madame was a thin little grey-haired woman of nearly seventy, with a brown face wrinkled like a walnut.   She laughed at the reluctant troops, went straight for the truck, grabbed the squealing pigs by the legs and whisked them out in a second.   A hearty cheer rewarded her, and the men formed up in procession behind her as she prodded their future Christmas dinner to its new home in the orchard.

For the next five weeks there wasn't much that was more important in the Battery than the welfare of its two pigs.   Gunner White mounted guard over them and understood that he was responsible for producing them in the right condition at the right

time. We christened them " Ack-Emma " (A.M.) and
" Pip-Emma " (P.M.). It became the favourite pastime
in the evening to lean over the sty and discuss their
points. Also to prod them, when Gunner White wasn't
looking. He took a serious view of his duties, and
objected to his charges being interfered with. In
addition, he grew quite fond of them. He became
quite jealous on rainy days when the ack-ack machine-
gunner in the orchard took shelter with his gun in the
sty.

As the weeks went by the Battery's enthusiasm
increased. It was aided by the splendid way in
which " Ack-Emma " and " Pip-Emma " fattened up.
Betting started on how much they would turn the
scale at when the day came. They cost practically
nothing to feed. Only the price of the bran. The
men's leavings provided the swill. It agreed with
them.

A week before Christmas a dreadful rumour spread.
The regiment was to move on Christmas Eve. We
didn't mind moving. But what about the pigs upon
which we had bestowed so much care and good swill ?
It would break the hearts of the Battery to leave them
behind. How could we take them with us ?

It resolved itself into the problem of pigs *versus*
equipment, and while the Pig Committee (the Major,
myself and N–Troop Commander) deliberated on ways
and means, the Battery went about on tip-toe.

" Hope ' Ack- ' and ' Pip-Emma ' aren't going to be
left out in the cold," said the gunners to the sergeants.
And " Hope ' Ack- ' and ' Pip-Emma ' aren't going to
be left out in the cold," said the sergeants to the
subalterns.

In the end, by dint of much juggling, we found
that we could put an entire regimental truck at the
disposal of " Ack " and " Pip-Emma." And the
Battery breathed freely again. And two days later

came the news that the regiment was not going to move, after all.

Next morning I happened to meet the Drag-Rope, L-Troop Leader, leaving the Mess with blanched face.

" What's the matter ? " I asked.

" I'm browned off," he almost hissed, meaning he was fed-up. " The Major's just detailed me to super-intend the slaughter of ' Ack ' and ' Pip-Emma.' Of course, it would be me."

" Cheer up," I said. " You couldn't expect that it was going to be a bloodless war for ever.

He went off, cursing his luck, to find moral support. The position was a bit complicated for him because Gunner White, expert on pigs from their origins to apple sauce, had just gone home on leave. So the Drag-Rope had to find a suitable deputy.

He gave long and careful thought to this, and finally selected Gunner Price, not without subtle reasons for so doing. Gunner Price had fought right through the last war. He sported the Mons Star among many other ribbons. He was one of the toughest fellows in the regiment. Here was one, thought the Drag-Rope, who would not quail at the sight of blood.

So together they took " Ack- " and " Pip-Emma " over to a village slaughter-house seven kilometres away, having first taken the Bren anti-aircraft gun out of the truck. The Liaison Officer had already made the arrangements with the municipal authorities.

When they arrived at the slaughter-house the doors were wide to receive them. There wasn't a soul to be seen in the village street except a little girl about eight years old, with golden hair and wide, innocent blue eyes—one of those pretty angel-face little girls.

She took one look at the pigs being transferred from the truck and shouted at the top of her voice :

" Quickly. Quickly. A pig's going to be killed."

Instantly all the children of the village, boys and

girls, swarmed out of cottages and side streets, and took up their position in orderly rows at the door of the slaughter-house, just like a theatre audience. The angel-faced little girl gave herself a front seat. They waited, breathless, for the curtain to go up.

The abbateurs strung " Ack- " and " Pip-Emma " up, amid much squealing, and seized their knives. The moment of execution had arrived.

It now occurred to the shaking Drag-Rope to look round for his moral support. But the veteran of 1914–18, the man who had been through the carnage of Mons, and the Somme, the tough guy, had vanished. The Drag-Rope discovered him outside, hiding behind the truck.

" Come along in," he said. " They'll probably want your assistance."

" I can't, sir ; I can't," was the hoarse reply. " The sight of blood affects me dreadful."

Nevertheless, he did manage to stagger back after the Drag-Rope to the slaughter-house.

A loud burst of hand-clapping from a delighted little audience accompanied the exit of " Ack-Emma." There followed another round of applause when " Pip-Emma " was dispatched.

Before this happened the Drag-Rope's moral support had again disappeared. He was holding on to the truck outside, white as a sheet, and shaking like a leaf.

" I can't stand it, sir ; I can't stand it," he groaned. " How them kids can do it ! "

" It's pretty awful," said the Drag-Rope, himself much shaken up. " Let's get back."

*   *   *   *   *

At dinner on Christmas Day the Battery solemnly declared that " Ack- " and " Pip-Emma " had fully repaid all the care and devotion bestowed on them.

The flesh was tender and tasty, and the crackling done to a turn.

In the evening when Y–Battery Mess embarked upon their share of the enjoyment, the Drag-Rope contrived to take a little of the edge off their appetites. He persisted in giving most gory and detailed descriptions of " Ack- " and " Pip-Emma's " last moments.

" Not at meal-time," we wailed.

But he was merciless. He felt he had something to pay off:

IX—FIRE AND FIREWORKS

The Major had Scotch blood in him. He never used six words when one would serve.

On this particular evening, however, it was more than Scotland that was biting him. During dinner he was taciturn. With the coffee and Benedictine he grew chatty as an oyster.

Also, the Mess itself had one of its moods on. About once a month, for no explicable reason, morbidity descended on us. It came without warning, and departed as suddenly. Nobody could forecast it. It just swam out of nothing. The symptoms were a gradual flickering-out of the conversation. Then someone would begin tapping the " Funeral March " (Chopin's) on the table. Somebody else twirled a table-knife to see who would be " first for it." Whomever the blade pointed at when the knife ceased revolving was the winner. Not a very cheerful pastime, though nobody took it seriously.

It was one of those evenings. At the first hint of Chopin the Major rose from the table.

" I'm going to my billet," he said, and departed.

We all knew what had upset him. The night before he had lost a truck. The Colonel had not been sympathetic. Moreover, the truck contained a very special high-power wireless set. So the Signal Officer must needs also fling up his hands.

The Major, driving the truck himself, had taken three other officers into Lille to spend a pleasant evening at the Café Metropole. The Café was the recognised rendezvous for all the troops, British and French, in the sector. Infantry, Cavalry, Artillery, Air Force, Engineers, Tanks, Supply Services, even Padres supplied their representatives to the crowd that packed the place out every evening. It provided much-needed social diversion on the grand scale for all units within a radius of thirty miles. And some thought it worth while to come farther than that. Here you ate oysters, very good and very cheap, in dozens. Here you sat for hours, chatting, and fascinated by the shifting, variegated throng. Here you met old friends who you didn't even know had been ordered to France. Here you made new friends and cemented the bonds with more oysters. It was a gay, exhilarating, swirling picture, the essence of military camaraderie. It might have been more colourful. The drab, stereotyped, khaki uniforms did nothing to attract the eye. But on top of this monotonous sea floated the bright hues of the " dress " forage caps of scores of different regiments. At least we were colourful from the head up.

At the Café Metropole, then, sat the Major in a state of peace with the world, though he was at war. Close to his elbow a group of Infantry officers were in open conversation. Anyone was welcome to listen, and anyone was welcome to join in. A captain began to talk:

" Can you beat this ? " he said. " I left my car, a Government Austin-Ten, in the square at Douai, locked up safely, while I went to do a bit of shopping. I was away about half an hour. Not more. I came back, unlocked it, and pressed the self-starter. Nothing happened. I had another go. Nothing happened. I went round and lifted the bonnet. The engine had gone. Solemn truth."

" That couldn't have been the L.A.D. " said one of his companions, incredulously.

" I'm not so sure. I wouldn't put it beyond them," observed the Captain, darkly.

" What about this ? " broke in a man who had

66

overheard. "Next regiment to us had a truck accident the other day. Bad skid, and crash into a tree. The driver was killed outright. His pal accompanied him in the ambulance. He was away about an hour. When he returned to the truck it had been gutted. Everything taken away that could be. Only the skeleton remained. Smart work that. Wonderful scroungers, the L.A.D."

Poor L.A.D. They were going through it again as they invariably did when the talk drifted in the direction of mysterious happenings to trucks. The L.A.D. are the Light Aid Detachment sections of the Royal Army Ordnance Corps attached to the various regiments. In a mechanised army their importance and utility is considerable. They, so to speak, are responsible for the general upkeep of the rolling stock of the regiment to which they are attached. It is a matter of professional pride with them to be able to supply spare parts at a minute's notice.

Now, rightly or wrongly, the L.A.D. were suspected of being utterly ruthless in the matter of keeping their stock of spares replete. They took what they wanted wherever they could find it, so the legend ran. You daren't leave a truck unattended by a lonely roadside for a quarter of an hour. Some L.A.D. might think it a wreck, and go in for " salvage," and you'd find the tyres gone, and the radiator missing. It was " scrounging " raised to the level of a fine art. I don't suggest for one moment that all the stories told about L.A.D. activities were true. They simply couldn't be. But the troops were very ready to believe them.

The Major listened idly to the conversation at the Café Metropole about the delinquencies of the L.A.D. It went on for some time, being a favourite Army topic. He'd heard it so often that he wasn't particularly interested. Finally the time came for

departure. He walked across to the Square where
he had parked his truck. It had vanished. He and
his companions had to hire a taxi to bring them home.

This misfortune, coming on top of one or two other
little troubles, worried the Major, who was a sensitive
man and extremely conscientious. When he walked
out of the Mess on this particular evening we all felt
sorry for him. So we had a few more drinks, and told
each other so.

At about nine o'clock there sounded a bit of a
commotion outside. Next moment, a breathless Don
R. (Despatch Rider) appeared in the doorway.

" The Wagon-Lines are on fire, sir," he announced.

Dead silence. We stared at each other. It was
unbelievable.

" What ? " I shouted.

" Wagon-Lines are on fire," he repeated.

In an instant we were alive.

" Get my truck ready, Hyde," I shouted to the
G.P.O. " Have another packed with all the fire
equipment you can lay your hands on. Harper, run
over to the M.O. and ask him to come along in case
he's needed. I'll tell the Major."

I dashed out of the door, ran across the road, and flew
up the stairs to the Major's room. He was standing in
front of the mirror in the act of taking off his tie.

" The Wagon-Lines are on fire, sir," I said.

He did not answer, but continued undressing. I
could see his expression in the mirror. It said :

" Poor fool. Fancy thinking I'd be taken in by
that one."

" They really are," I assured him.

He swung round and saw that I was in earnest.
And now his expression said :

" Good God ! This . . . on top of everything else."

In half a minute we were out of the billet and across
to where the trucks were warming up.

The Wagon-Lines were at Moncheux, six miles away.

" I hope those men are safe," said the Major, anxiously, as we tore along in the darkness.

I knew the men he was referring to, and suffered the same anxiety. There was a big straw barn at the farmhouse where the Wagon-Lines were installed, It was about forty feet high, and as capacious as a couple of good-sized houses. This was crammed with straw from floor to floor, all built up in great separate cubes. Being a bit overcrowded a dozen of the gunners had provided themselves with a most ingenious billet by removing some of these cubes. A narrow passage led to the heart of the rick of compressed straw, where two large " rooms " had been constructed something in the style of an Eskimo igloo. The gunners had rigged up electric light with the help of a wire from the adjoining farmhouse. In this remarkable dug-out they could afford to laugh at the wet and the cold. The order, of course, was " No smoking," and " No naked lights."

My mind had flown to that straw barn the instant I heard the Wagon-Lines were ablaze. And the same thought occupied the Major, with all its dreadful possibilities.

We had something else to dread. All our reserve ammunition, tons and tons of shells and charges, was stored at the Wagon-Lines. If that went up . . . Well, we tried not to think about it.

As we topped the crest of the hill at Versay we had our first glimpse of the conflagration. What a blaze. The red glow illuminated the sky for miles around. And when we reached Moncheux soon after, we found what we expected. The straw barn was one colossal, towering furnace, spouting great tongues of flame at the dark sky. You couldn't get anywhere near it, the heat was so terrific.

L-Troop Commander, who with about a hundred men was billeted at the Wagon-Lines, was shouting the necessary orders for the removal of the regimental vehicles to a place of safety. The men had already flung themselves on the seventeen tons of high explosives stored in a lean-to shed in the orchard, and all of it was now beyond reach of mischief. The trailers containing ammunition had likewise been moved a couple of hundred yards down the road. There was no danger of a big bang, thanks to the swift, vigorous action of the Troop Commander and his men.

The Troop Commander came up, red, grimy, and sweating from his exertions.

" All the men safe ? " asked the Major.

" I think so, sir."

" Call the roll."

There was a brief halt in the operations while the Troop-Sergeant-Major called the roll. Everyone answered to his name except Gunner Jones.

" Gunner Jones ! " roared the Sergeant-Major, and his roar could be heard above the roar of the flames.

No answer. Twice more the Sergeant-Major boomed forth. Still no reply.

" Anyone seen Gunner Jones since the fire started ? " cried the Major.

Silence.

" Find him," said the Major, laconically.

So small search parties were detailed off to comb all the barns, farm-buildings, and outhouses for the missing man.

" Looks bad," said the Major, gravely, and gazing at the fiery furnace across the courtyard we all experienced a very uncomfortable sensation.

Meanwhile the local fire brigade had arrived ; three men manning a hand-pump, the water supply being the small duck-pond opposite the farmhouse. They pumped vigorously but only a thin trickle of water

left the hose. Things improved, however, when some
of our investigating gunners removed three wicker-
baskets and a coil of rope from the bottom of the
tank. Even then it was pretty evident that the fire
brigade was not going to worry the blaze very much.
The straw-barn roared away unchecked.

Suddenly the cry went up :

"Gunner Jones found. Gunner Jones found."

He had been discovered in one of the other barns.
And, amidst all the noise, turmoil, and shouting going
on around, he had been discovered fast asleep.

I hope we were not ungrateful. We really did feel
a tremendous relief that he was safe. But, at the
same time, there was hardly a man in the Wagon-
Lines who did not resent the anxiety Gunner Jones
had unnecessarily imposed upon him. That he had
been safe asleep all the time seemed to add insult to
injury. Such is human nature.

Human nature was now displaying itself in other
respects. There were five occupants of the farmhouse
which now seemed in grave danger of sharing the fate
of the straw-barn, to which it was linked by other
farm buildings. The farmer himself, a French reservist about forty-five years old, had only returned home
on leave six hours before. He had come straight from
a long spell in the Maginot Line. What his feelings
were may be guessed. But like a good soldier he kept
them to himself, and devoted his energies to helping
the British soldiers who were striving to save his
home. His short, khaki-clad steel-helmeted figure was
to the fore wherever work was to be done. Beyond
an occasional suggestion barely a word escaped his lips.

Not so his wife, a dark strong beady-eyed woman of
about the same age. The fire released from her a
torrent of indignant wrath, and all the words to
express it in. The poor Troop Commander had to
bear the full brunt of it. From the moment the fire

started she seemed to labour under the impression that he was burning down her farmhouse on purpose. She followed him about all the time, shouting at him and shaking her fists in his face. The Troop Commander was a cool hand in any emergency. But fire-fighting, with a hysterical woman on his tail every minute, abusing and threatening him, and distracting him, was worse than a barrage. She stuck to him like a leech, aided and abetted by a grown-up daughter who, when her mother did get stuck for a word, supplied a dozen.

It had its ludicrous side (to the onlookers), especially when the sweating, exhausted Troop Commander tried sweet reason. He endeavoured to explain to the frantic woman : (1) That he was due to go home on leave the next day. (2) That there was nothing in the world he wanted so much as leave. (3) That because of the fire his leave would have to be postponed.

" Therefore, madame, is it likely I should have done it on purpose ? "

Pretty, but utterly useless in the circumstances. The only effect was to send madame off into a fresh outburst. She now insisted that as the Troop Commander might be going on leave so soon, he must pay on the spot the money for the damage. He had a hard time explaining that she would have to wait.

The other two occupants of the farm, the farmer's aged mother and father, supplied the dignified pathos required as contrast to the hysteria of Madame. They sat with folded hands by the side of the pile of furniture removed for safety from the living-rooms to the orchard. They never uttered a word as they watched the flames eating into their home. These same flames lit up their wrinkled faces, full of tragedy now, but brave. The faces of people who, in a long life, had become inured to misfortune and disaster, and now faced a fresh one like Stoics.

By now troops from miles round had arrived to

offer assistance, including the M.O.s of all the neighbouring regiments. A sergeant of the Security Police came along to find out if we had any suspicions that the fire was caused by enemy agents. We hadn't.

It now became obvious that the only way to save the residential part of the farm from destruction was to cut the building in two. The farmer saw the necessity and agreed. Soon the gunners were swarming over the roof with pickaxes, saws and crowbars.

This new phase brought, as it happened, long-prayed for and much-needed relief to the oppressed Troop Commander. The sight of the crowbars at work proved the last straw for Madame. The poor overwrought woman opened her mouth to shout protests. But her voice had completely gone. She collapsed under the strain, and the M.O. had to dose her with sedatives. It says a lot for the Troop Commander that when he suddenly missed the sound of the voice that had been his terror for three solid hours, and was told what had happened, he found time among all the urgency of the moment to say :

" Poor old thing. I hope she'll be all right."

We cut a gap ten feet wide in the building, played the hose on it steadily, and left the straw-barn to burn itself out. It was half-past three in the morning before the fire was conquered.

*   *   *   *   *

Things are found out in the Army, sometimes, with a speed and certainty that would arouse the admiration of Scotland Yard. It was so a few hours later, when the Court of Inquiry into the circumstances of the fire discovered that the person responsible was none other than Gunner Jones, the man who had given us so much anxiety when the roll was called. Gunner Jones, it appeared, had developed a fancy for solitude at night. He was in the habit of leaving

73

his billet and climbing up to the top of the straw-barn to sleep. On this fatal night, however, when he came to walk along the top of the straw to his usual couch, he suddenly found nothing under his feet, and dropped about twelve feet into the centre. Unbeknown to him, the farmer during the day had removed a couple of big cubes of straw from the centre.

When Gunner Jones fell, a lighted candle end fell with him. It dropped out of his hand and disappeared down a crack between two of the bales of straw where he could not reach it. However, it seemed to have extinguished itself all right. But his fall had given him a dislike to his usual sleeping accommodation, so he went over to another barn and was soon wrapped in slumber so sound that it took a search party to waken him.

All of which was duly recorded.

*　　　　*　　　　*　　　　*　　　　*

What wasn't recorded was the miserable life spent for the ensuing weeks by the Troop Commander and his lieutenant down at the Wagon-Lines. Every time they showed their faces near the farmhouse out came Madame and her daughter to insist on being paid there and then for the damage done to their farm. They could not understand why " the rich British Army " were not able to pay at once. The Troop Commander tried to explain that the damage would be assessed by an officer of the Royal Engineers, and a claim would be sent in, and Madame would get the money without any doubt. And then another long argument started.

Finally the daughter took to cycling over to Head-quarters at Auchy in the morning before breakfast to see if the money had arrived.

This was more than a joke. So we gave it to the Liaison Officer to straighten out.

74

X—The Backward Baby Intervenes

Y–Battery had never seen the L.A.D. Officer's baby. The L.A.D. Officer himself had never seen it. In fact, nobody had seen it. For the simple reason that it was yet to be born.

Yet there came a time when this unborn infant shared with Herr Hitler the distinction of exerting considerable influence on the immediate affairs of certain of the members of Y–Battery mess.

This is how it happened.

We were now deep in November. Deep is the right word, in view of the sea of mud and water through which we waded, going about our daily duties. It rained, rained, rained. If it stopped for an hour, it was only to give the sky a chance to prepare another jugful. We were fast developing into some amphibious species. And when we took off our gum-boots at the end of a long day it felt like shedding part of one's natural hide. In the gun-pits the water made respectable lakes.

" I shouldn't be surprised if there's fish in them," said Tops one gloomy afternoon. " I'll write home and ask them to send out my tackle."

To such depths of optimism had we sunk.

Suddenly the rain stopped ; the waters receded ; the earth became dry. (It didn't really, but henceforth our minds were fixed on other things.)

One word wrought this miracle—and that word was LEAVE.

It began as a rumour, and instantly everybody was seized with a colossal craving to see, and be seen of,

Old England again. Rumour fattened into fact. Finally at five o'clock one evening after R.H.Q. conference, representatives from the two batteries met in the Colonel's office to draw lots for leave.

First name out of the petrol tin was Turner's, the L.A.D. Officer. That meant he would be home for Christmas, and we flooded him with congratulations. Much to our surprise, he did not appear at all pleased. If anything, put out. Then our attention was distracted by the discovery that somebody was going to be Number Thirteen. And as luck would have it, the lot fell on me.

" You'll soon be nudging mines," exclaimed Tops cheerfully.

But I wasn't superstitious. " Thirteen suits me better than fourteen," I said.

Some days before the L.A.D. Officer was due to go on leave an astonishing thing occurred. He walked up to Yeates in the mess one evening and said rather diffidently :

" I've been looking at the leave rota, and see you're down for January 10. Would you care to swop leaves with me ? "

" It's yours," exclaimed Yeates without any delay. " But, I say, why aren't you using it yourself ? "

" Oh, er—private reasons," replied the L.A.D. Officer, a trifle confused—and walked out.

When Yeates told us we could hardly credit it. Not want to be home for Christmas when you had the chance ! The man must be wandering.

Next day, when I met Turner, I said : " I'm down for January 22. If you're swopping leave again, remember me."

I intended it as a joke, but the L.A.D. Officer took me quite seriously.

" Let me see," he reflected, " you were thirteen, weren't you ? Thanks awfully, but I don't think I'll swop with you."

Next thing I heard was that when the L.A.D. Officer again became due for leave he did a deal with the Babe. All in the same " private and confidential " way. By now Y–Battery Mess felt face to face with the Incomprehensible. We also had (except myself) the exciting sensation that at any moment our leave might be jumped forward, through the inexplicable agencies of the L.A.D. It was a fine set-off to the ever-present dread that our leaves might be indefinitely put back at any moment by the equally obscure designs of Herr Hitler.

At last, when the L.A.D. Officer negotiated a third swop with a G.P.O. of Z–Battery, we could bear it no longer. We sat him down in a chair in the mess and mounted guard over him till he talked.

The explanation was very simple. The L.A.D.'s wife was expecting a baby. They had arranged that he should time his leave so as not to waste any of it before that event happened. But there had been some mistake in the calculations. The baby did not seem to be forthcoming when expected. You know how these things are. The L.A.D. Officer kept in constant communication with his wife. According to the nature of her bulletins, so he studied the leave rota. And at least three of the regiment had reason to thank the backwardness of the L.A.D. Officer's baby.

*   *   *   *   *

Meanwhile, Number Thirteen began to pay me attention. I contracted a dreadful chill through sleeping in a soaking billet. The regiment was about to move forward from Auchy to Armentieres, right on the Belgian frontier. I had to be in the open a lot. And the weather changed to bitter cold. At last the

M.O. insisted on taking me in hand. Bronchitis was his verdict, and instant bed his order.

Fortunately I had a jewel of a billet at Armentieres in a splendid mansion belonging to M. Guillaume, a wealthy mill-owner. He and his charming wife did all they could to make my purgatory endurable. But they couldn't remove the dread ever haunting me— that I'd be too ill to go on leave when my turn came. The day came nearer and nearer. The M.O. shook his head every visit. I grew resigned to losing my turn. Then happened one of our monthly " flaps " (invasion scares). All leave was cancelled indefinitely, and I was in the running again. And it was my turn next.

On my first evening up, very groggy indeed, I crawled down to the mess. The Colonel was dining with us. After dinner he said very kindly to me :

" Look here, if you like to go on leave when I go, directly after this scare is over, I'll give you a lift in my car to Boulogne. It'll make it more comfortable and less tiring for you."

" Thanks very much, sir," I replied gratefully. And just then a Don R. brought along a message from R.H.Q. saying that leave was renewed as from to-morrow.

The Colonel decided to catch the eight o'clock boat in the morning, and forgetting I was just out of bed after a bad illness, said : " Meet me at my garage at 3 a.m."

I snatched a couple of hours' sleep in the mess, got my servant to pack my kit, and struggled along to the garage in a heavy snowstorm. We journeyed up the frontier to Bailleul, turned right at Cassel, then to St. Omer, the snow falling so thick that at times visibility shrank to four yards. I lay back in the car, cold, exhausted, and weak after my long spell

of slops. A dim thought began to shape itself in my
mind that I hadn't yet done with Thirteen.

A snow-drift brought the car to a dead stop. We
dug it out—that is, the Colonel, his servant, and the
driver—with spades borrowed from a near-by farmhouse, to reach which we pushed through snow breast
high. A snow-plough working between two villages
came along and we followed it as far as it went. By
now there was no chance of catching the 8 a.m. boat
from Boulogne. However, we decided to press on.
The snow was thicker than ever. A great white
blanket covered the country-side and a piercing east
wind raked the road.

Two miles further on we plunged into another drift,
with the snow up to the windscreen in front and
packed all round the windows so that we looked to
be in an ice-box. This time we were rescued by some
French soldiers, who pushed the car into Harlette, a
village thirty kilometres from Boulogne.

There was no longer hope of going forward. The
drifts choked the roads. We began to think of food
—or, rather, the Colonel did. I was hungry enough,
but my stomach was weak and fastidious ; and the
delicacies that would have tempted me weren't likely
to be found in Harlette. The only estaminet in the
village had been commandeered by a company of
French infantry, who were doing their cooking there.
Cold rabbit pie was all they had to offer us. The
Colonel said it was delicious. I take his word for it.
One look at it was enough for me in my sick state.

The room was packed with poilus, singing songs,
smoking the inevitable Caporal cigarettes, and spitting
all over the floor. A thick haze of blue smoke sent
me into a fit of coughing Round the stove huddled
a ring of soldiers, keeping what little heat it did
provide away from everybody else. Every time the
door swung open a blast of cold air blew in, driving

the snowflakes before it ; and they melted into muddy pools on the floor. I shivered and shivered.

" This is what comes of drawing Number Thirteen," I thought dejectedly. Then I had a couple of cognacs, and that braced me up to continue the struggle. After all, the prize was worth it—Leave. And England.

Then things brightened. Le Capitaine Duval, of the 137th Infantry, appeared, introduced himself to the Colonel, and promised to find us a billet for the night.

" And, messieurs, will you do me the honour of dining with me in our mess ? "

We certainly would. Anything to get out of the reek of that estaminet.

It was a small Company mess in a little room in a farmhouse, lit by an oil-lamp. There were Captain Duval, a lieutenant, the adjutant (equivalent to our sergeant-major) and three sous-lieutenants (N.C.O.s.). They smothered me with kindness and sympathy when the Colonel explained that I was ill. They made me sit by the stove, plied me with hot coffee, as I couldn't eat anything, gave me aspirin tablets, and finally the lieutenant made me an " honorary " member of the regiment by pinning on my tunic their regimental badge. He delivered the neatest and politest of little speeches to grace this ceremony. And I remember how angry and ashamed I felt that I was too ill to do more than stand up unsteadily and mutter " Thank you."

At half-past ten the Colonel and I departed for the billet, which proved to be a stable with an earth floor, furnished with an iron double-bed and a table. The wind whistled through the cracks, the door had a broken hinge, and the cold was petrifying. For days the temperature had never been higher than twenty-five degrees of frost, and to-night it was colder than ever.

The Colonel regarded me apprehensively.

"I'm not taking much off," I said. "Only my blouse and boots. And I'll get into my flea-bag."

"Good idea," said the Colonel. But priding himself on being a bit of a Spartan, he undressed to his vest and pants.

We hopped into bed, turned back to back, and said good night.

In the middle of the night I was aroused from my aspirin slumber by a violent shaking of the bed. I traced it to the Colonel. As I stirred he spoke :

"Are you warm ? " he asked.

"Very," I replied. "Are you ? "

"I'm frozen stiff," he said.

"Put some more clothes on," I suggested.

The cold had beaten even him. He hopped out of bed, dressed, and jumped back into bed again. And so we passed the night.

In the morning the snow had ceased. A military snow-plough came from Boulogne to clear the road. After lunch we were able to make a fresh start.

Number Thirteen was now very much in the ascendant, so far as I was concerned. I felt so groggy that the nearer we drew to Boulogne the farther away my leave seemed to retreat. My shiverings assumed gigantic proportions. I could see the Colonel watching me out of the corner of his eye, with concern on his face. This unsettled me more than ever. The Colonel was never the man to show concern unless things were going very badly indeed.

As we skidded into the centre of Boulogne a large French naval funeral held us up. I saw five coffins surrounded by a company of French sailors. So weak and dizzy was I, that I thought for the moment I was seeing things in a sort of semi-delirium. It was one coffin, and I was seeing five.

"How many coffins do you see, sir ? " I asked the Colonel.

" Five," he replied.

" I'm glad of that ! " I exclaimed, much relieved.

He gave me a queer look.

The Colonel put me straight to bed at the hotel, ordered me hot drinks, and went out to buy me aspirin and cough mixture. Also he had business down at the quay concerning the morning boat. I lay in bed haunted by Number Thirteen. What a business ! Would it beat me after all ? I had visions of myself, having got thus far towards leave and England, being carted off to hospital and left behind. The prospect roused me to desperation. Damn it, I'll have my leave in face of all the Thirteens in the world ! I rang for hot soup, and commenced ladling it down my throat direct from the tureen.

Perhaps it was good food I was in need of after my long diet of slops. Anyhow, when I awoke next morning I was much steadier and stronger. Able to travel, which was all that mattered.

The Colonel drove the car right up to the gangway of the leave boat on the quayside. I nipped on board. Then I found that the previous evening, with me in mind, he had arranged to be O.C. ship, which gave him the use of a private cabin, on the couch of which I dozed in comfort as we crossed the Channel. Good-bye, Thirteen, I exulted.

*   *   *   *   *

And then : Dover . . . train . . . Victoria . . . Home . . . bed . . . hot-water bottles . . . doctor . . . temperature 103 . . . " in bed for at least a week. . . ."

My head started to buzz with figures.

" Ten days' leave. . . . Seven from ten leaves three. . . . Ten and three . . . Ten and three. . . ."

Why, continually, ten and three ? Ah, yes, I remembered at last.

Ten plus three makes—THIRTEEN !

BATTLE

I—FOURTEEN HOURS TO BEGIN WITH

" Did you pick this décor for our première, Babe ? "
asked Tops, N–Troop Commander, with suspicious
absence of guile.

" Why ? " said the Babe warily. He knew from
experience that his artistic leanings, especially his
youthful passion for the Russian ballet, provided the
Troop Commander with his favourite subject for chaff
in off moments.

" Well, I think it's just too, too sweet," drawled the
Troop Commander. " I suppose some of your Russian
ballet pals pulled strings at Corps H.Q. So here we
are. You know. L'Après-midi d'un Faune, isn't it ? "

He ducked with a laugh, and the empty sardine tin
that the Babe pitched, tangented off the side of his
tin hat into the long grass.

Y–Battery Mess had just concluded a rough-and-
ready lunch off stew and hard cheese, and we were all
rather sleepy. With only one halt the regiment had
raced all the way from Havre to our present position,
sixteen miles or so west of Brussels. After hanging
about on the Belgian frontier for months, ready to
dart in the moment the Germans moved, it would be
just our luck for the invasion to start when we were
miles and miles away, preparing to embark for Norway.
So we had come helter-skelter back from Havre; into
Belgium at Tournai, and up through Renaix to the
village of Neder Brakel a few miles west of the
canalised River Dendre, where a halt was called, and
the guns and vehicles went into a " hide " in a large
orchard. We were, in fact, enveloped in orchards.

85

Y–Battery Mess had been laid out under apple trees, with their marvellous fresh green leafage making a much needed umbrella against the burning noon sun. The place looked much too idyllic for battle, and the Troop Commander was not far wrong in his description. In an adjacent field a Bofors continued pom-pomming away at stray Messerschmitts. We had grown very used to that in the eight months prelude to the invasion. Therefore it contributed little to destroy the illusion that the beauty of the orchards, with the sunshine dappling the grass beneath, created.

The Hooker, L–Troop Commander, burly, six-foot-two, and of Rugby scrum prowess, parted his eyelids.

"Did I hear somebody suggest we're going into action?" he inquired, sleepily. "No such luck. I can't believe it after all these months. In an hour or so we'll be on the move again. My young hopes have been blighted too often."

"I'll take ten to one it's action," said N–Troop G.P.O. (Gun Position Officer). "On second thoughts, I won't. It would be petty theft."

"What do you know?" his Troop Commander objected.

"All I know," replied the G.P.O. calmly, "is that the great moments of my life always happen just when I can't get the full fun out of them because I'm so dog-tired I want to go to sleep. And at this present moment I simply can't keep awake."

And so saying, the G.P.O. toppled gently off his canvas folding-chair on to the grass, and instantly went to sleep.

"What a prophet!" laughed the Troop Commander.

Nevertheless, the G.P.O. was right. Half an hour later along came the Colonel to take the two O.P. (Observation Post) officers of Y–Battery, the Hooker and myself, on a reconnaissance of O.P.'s. The Major accompanied us. Meanwhile the Second-in-Command went off with the three G.P.O.'s and the Command Post Officer to choose the Troop gun positions.

It was real business at last.

The main army that had been heavily engaged around Brussels was now falling back in good order, their withdrawal being covered by the 25th Infantry Brigade and some Guards' battalions, who were holding bridgeheads over the Dendre at Ninove. Our two batteries of twenty-five pounders were supporting the rearguard. It was our job to help to cover the withdrawal of the main forces, and afterwards the retirement of the rearguard.

From our " hide " among the orchards we started off to find suitable O.P.'s, driving our trucks forward along a sunken road for a distance of two miles. Streaming in the opposite direction flowed the tide of civilian refugees from the Brussels countryside. Out of side roads and lanes they trickled like tributaries to swell the main river. All manner of household belongings that could be moved were piled upon all manner of wheeled vehicles—cars, carts, cycles, perambulators, wheelbarrows—anything that could be driven, pedalled, pushed or pulled. The people who hadn't wheels to assist them, carried what they could on their backs. Even small children stumbled along under their burdens. It was a tide of humanity at its saddest.

After pushing through them for a couple of miles we halted, left our trucks, and climbed a bank to the top of a slope where some defensive trenches had been dug by the Belgians long before the invasion. They were unoccupied, and commanded a good field of fire over a wide stretch of rolling country, dotted here and there with small woods, right away to the enemy front line. Cross-roads, distant groups of houses, and other landmarks stood out pretty distinct. From the O.P. officer's point of view it was an ideal spot for conducting harassing-fire and counter-preparation tasks ; in other words, shelling the enemy as they advanced, or smashing them up when they were making preparations for attack under cover of woods and houses.

" This will do fine," said the Colonel, lowering his glasses. He went on to point out our zone. " You will observe and take on targets presenting themselves from that church over there to the right end of that wood, inclusive."

It was a big zone—90 degrees—and couldn't be properly observed from one O.P. So we travelled up the road for another mile and picked on a second, a red-brick farmhouse on the brow of a rise. The old farmer, his wife, and two sons were still working in the fields.

" By the way," added the Colonel, " I want you to see if you can cover the main road leading out of Brussels on the extreme left of the zone. If necessary, find a third O.P. It won't be permanently manned. Just in case it's needed."

With that he said good-bye and returned to the " hide " to reconnoitre Z–Battery's O.P.'s.

The Major, the Hooker and I set about finding the provisional O.P. It wasn't an easy job, but eventually we decided on a mound at a road junction from which a good stretch of the Brussels road was visible. We halted our trucks on a rough track, and were walking back across the two fields separating us from the farm-house when anti-aircraft shells began to burst over our heads. A Messerschmitt was coming up behind us, only a hundred feet above. So we made a quick dive into the nearest ditch, and crouched down while the plane sprayed our trucks with machine-gun bullets. It disappeared with the ack-ack shells bursting round it in the blue cloudless sky.

"You take the farmhouse O.P.," said the Major to me. He went off back to the battery, the Hooker departed to his O.P. in the trenches, and, with the help of a Number 7 Director, range-finder, artillery board, and my O.P. Ack, I settled down to the business of doing a silent registration, taking the switches, ranges, and angles of sight of possible targets in the zone, and also drawing a panorama of the zone and filling it with the necessary data, identifying positions such as churches, woods, farmhouses and hamlets.

Half-way through this long job, German bombers began heavily bombing a road junction two miles distant. My seat on top of the slope gave me a grandstand view. The guns on the ground were giving the Germans a hot time. One plane received a direct hit, burst into flames, fell from the sky trailing a black wake, and crashed into a wood, from which, a few seconds later there streamed up in the windless air a tall, vertical pillar of smoke. The swift drama fascinated me so much that I continued staring at the dark, rigid colum rising straight into the sky like some strange, mournful monolith.

Suddenly I heard the O.P. Ack's voice:

"Blimey, sir! Look! Here's the finish of the Gran' National."

I looked, and saw that it was quite likely going to be the finish of us. Three black Messerschmitts were out doing a bit of hedge-hopping. They cleared the hedge about two hundred yards in front, flying fifteen feet from the ground, coming straight at us.

There was no time for words. Stooping low, we raced for the nearest barn, and flung ourselves flat in the dark interior. The farmer, his wife, and his sons had already arrived and were lying on their faces, almost invisible. As I went down I heard the O.P. Ack fall with a grunt, and exclaim hoarsely ;

" Pardong, merdame. Pardong, s'il vous play."

Then, breathless silence within the barn, while outside the machine-guns of the Messerschmitts rattled away, and the bullets panged against the walls of the buildings.

After half a minute the storm blew over. We picked ourselves up, no damage done. Walking back to resume our registration, the O.P. Ack said :

" That was a close shave for me, sir, no mistake."

At first I thought he was referring to the close shave we had all shared with him. But he wasn't bothering about the Messerschmitts.

" I came near as nothing to falling slap on top of the old girl in that barn," he said.

We hadn't yet finished with our Messerschmitts. Five minutes later they suddenly swept round the side of a small wood behind the farmhouse. But this time they had other objects in view, and apart from a couple of short bursts of machine-gun fire at the farmhouse by way of farewell they troubled us not at all. It was an unfortunate village about three miles to the left that claimed their worst attentions. We heard the terrific explosion of the bombs, and clouds of dust and smoke filled the air.

Stew again and fruit salad awaited me for supper when I returned to the " hide " as dusk was falling, with a panorama of the zone that was quite a work of art. As soon as darkness hid us from observation the guns were dragged out to their positions, and the gunners started digging the pits. Y–Battery were on the outskirts of a small village called Aspelaere. L–Troop guns occupied the back gardens of a row of small cottages up a lane leading off to the right from the big road that ran east towards Brussels. In front of them, for some six hundred yards, stretched corn-fields with a wood beyond. M–Troop guns were on the far side of this wood, with N–Troop a quarter of a mile to their left, on the other side of the Brussels road. Thus the battery formed a rough triangle, with L–Troop guns as the apex.

As dawn broke, the British divisions that had been engaged in the battle round Brussels came pouring past us along the roads—long lines of trucks crowded with tired infantry, Bren-gun carriers, artillery regiments with shell-scarred tractors, and ambulances. Throughout the day, and the ensuing night, they continued to rumble along on their way to take up new positions behind us on the line of the Escaut. For Y–Battery the morning and afternoon passed quietly enough, enlivened only by a fight between a couple of Spitfires and a Messerschmitt, which dived straight towards L–Troop position in its efforts to escape. The guns and gun-pits were sprayed by the bullets from the Spitfires. But no one was hit, and the Messerschmitt crashed about a thousand yards away.

As the afternoon wore away I began to feel surprised that no orders had come to man the O.P.'s we had so conscientiously reconnoitred the day before. But I was more than surprised when I discovered that the Major had departed to reconnoitre and man a new one, taking with him the Hooker. He had received a 'phone message from the Colonel to say that the first two O.P.'s were no good. The pace of the withdrawal was quicker than had been anticipated, and there was every likelihood that they would be overrun by the enemy while being used. So one had to be found in an area farther back.

Now I considered O.P. work my speciality; and for months had promised myself the pleasure of conducting the Y–Battery's first shoot against the enemy.

I was awaiting the Major at the Battery Command Post when he returned. He could see from my face what I was thinking.

"Now don't get sore about it," he said, with a grin. "I know you'd like to have gone. But you happen to be second-in-command, and I must keep you here with the Battery in case anything happens to me. In any case, he won't be there long. He's got to get back before the bridge-heads are blown up. And that's only a matter of a few hours."

He was so kind about it that I couldn't cherish my grievance. Besides, the Hooker deserved every inch of his luck.

The new O.P. was just over the far bank of the Dendre, close up to the infantry. The Major had impressed upon the Hooker that he must vacate it and cross the river before the time arranged for the bridge-heads to be blown up or he'd be cut off.

It was getting on towards seven in the evening. A hush of expectancy enveloped the Battery. I strolled over to L–Troop Command Post for a chat with the G.P.O. He was located with his telephone operator in the top back room of one of the cottages, about thirty yards from the guns.

"Why aren't you at the O.P. after drawing such a pretty picture of it ? " was his greeting.

"The Hooker's doing the shooting," I replied, shortly. "And at any moment the show may start."

Hardly had I spoken when the telephone rang. It was the Battery Command Post in the cellar of a farmhouse three-quarters of a mile away, sending down the fire orders.

The telephone operator, receivers clamped to his ears, began to write on a pad of paper. Over his shoulder hung the G.P.O. and I, watching.

"Fresh Target . . ." wrote the operator, and the

G.P.O. dashed to the open window, thrust his head out, and shouted :

" Take Post ! "

Below the gun-crews jumped to their positions. The telephone operator continued to write. As he did so the G.P.O. bawled the orders from the window :

" Fresh target. . . . H.E. 117. . . . Charge 3. . . . Zero 5 degrees. . . .Angle of sight, 15' elevation. . . . Fire by order. . . . 6,800 (range). . . . 10 rounds per gun per hour. . . . Irregular intervals. . . ."

Down in the back gardens the No. 1's on the guns saluted in acknowledgment of the orders. In the quiet evening came the clang, clang, clang, clang of the breeches of the four guns, slammed-to behind the charges by the No. 2's. Then, from the No. 1's :

" Number Three gun ready, sir . . ."

" Number One gun ready, sir . . ."

" Number Two gun ready, sir . . ."

" Number Four gun ready, sir . . ."

Not a bit otherwise than as a practice shoot on Salisbury Plain, though this *was* the real thing. Just as orderly and methodical. It was difficult to realise that, after all these months of waiting, our first shells would soon be on their way to the enemy.

There followed a pause of a few minutes, almost unbroken by the slightest sound, within or without. The G.P.O. kept his eyes glued to the operator's pad. Then the telephone tinkled again, and the pencil resumed writing :

" FIRE ! . . ."

" FIRE ! . . ." yelled the G.P.O. through the window, and our twenty-five-pounders roared in battle for the first time.

I don't know what effect those shells had upon the enemy, miles away. But the results close at hand were quite unexpected. Every cow in the neighbour-hood began to moo loudly in terror, flocks of sheep bleated, pigs grunted as they had never grunted before, scores of dogs barked violently without a break, and the women who had remained till now in their cottages supported by a fatalistic calm, rushed out of doors screaming. The entire district was roused to pandemonium. It was also roused to flight. The villagers sadly accepted our salvo as the signal that their time to be homeless had come. As the twilight drew on another pathetic little procession dribbled down the lane to join the main stream of fugitives on the road leading westward.

Hour by hour our gunfire continued with its automatic irregularity. By half-past nine the long evening was beginning to show signs of nightfall. I picked up the telephone to have a chat with the Battery Command Post. Hogan, the Assistant C.P.O.—an international golfer—answered, so I asked him how he was enjoying this round.

" We are awfully worried here," he surprised me by saying.

" What's up ? "

" We're afraid something nasty has happened to the Hooker. We can't get in touch with him at all. His wireless has been dead for over half an hour."

" D'you think he's been cut off ? "

" Looks like it. The bridgeheads should have been blown up by now."

This was indeed bad news. The Hooker and I had been together in the regiment for nearly ten years, and our friendship was firm. The thought that I might not be seeing him again left me for a moment or two without words.

" We'll have to do the rest of our firing from the map," I heard the A.C.P.O. saying.

" Yes," I replied. " Look, old fellow. Ring me up if you get any news of him, won't you ? "

Then I put down the telephone and went for a walk

round the gun-pits to take my mind off unpleasant possibilities.

It was now quite dark. The flashes from the gun muzzles lit up the night intermittently. We were now firing on prearranged targets from the map. Apart from the gun flashes, nothing disturbed the blackness from now on, except the faint glow of the illuminating apparatus hovering over the dial sights whenever the guns were laid on new targets. One gun crew was rested every hour, and in the G.P.O.'s Command Post we took it in turns to snatch fragments of difficult, uneasy sleep on the straw-covered floor.

Just about midnight I had a telephone call from the Battery Command Post. It was the A.C.P.O.

" Thought you'd like to know there's a rumour going round that the Hooker was seen swimming across the canal," he said.

" Did he get across ? " I asked.

" Don't know. I can't find out where the rumour comes from. Expect it has been picked up from the infantry. They're coming through pretty thick now. Let you know if I hear any more. Sleep well."

It wasn't very comforting, but it seemed more preferable than blank silence. At least, I did know that the Hooker was a strong swimmer. The Dendre wouldn't give him any trouble. Yes, there was some comfort in the rumour. In those early days we had not yet learned that the one thing in our immediate world wherein it was best not to find either comfort or discomfort, was Rumour.

At 2.30 a.m. the telephone again rang, and again it was the A.C.P.O.

" Switch off the anxiety," he shouted cheerily. " The Hooker has just arrived. Looks as though he's been in the scrum of his life. Offer him a hot bath. He's coming up to see you as soon as the Major has finished with him."

95

So that was that. And I suddenly found myself very wide awake and humming a tune loud enough to cause the G.P.O. to suggest ironically that perhaps it might be better for all parties concerned if he continued his forty winks in one of the gun-pits.

Soon after the Hooker appeared, very tired, very dusty, and looking rather crestfallen for six-foot-two. While he drenched himself with cups of syrupy ebony tea supplied from the gunners' cook-house, he related his woes. His O.P. had been in a field at the end of a hedge by a five-barred gate. Here he stationed himself with his wireless operator and his O.P. Ack, leaving his truck and driver some four hundred yards in the rear. (You never take your truck right up to the O.P.) The Hooker settled down to his job, and time passed very quickly and pleasantly, till, suddenly looking round the corner of the hedge to see if there was anything new worth sending down to the Battery as a target, he was staggered to see a detachment of German infantry advancing towards him across the fields, only fifty yards away. Swiftly and painfully it dawned upon him that the British infantry had retired without him knowing. He yelled to his companions to run for the truck, stayed behind long enough to kick his wireless set to pieces (he knew how to make a good job of that all right!), and then followed, firing his revolver at the enemy as he ran. Meanwhile some of our own infantry who had taken up a line between him and his truck, mistook him in the fading light for a German, and opened fire on him. He managed to get safely to the truck, and the party tore off to the banks of the Dendre, only to find that the nearest bridgehead had been blown up. The same had happened to the next, and the third was on the point of going up when the Hooker's truck appeared. He just had time to get across, joined the retreating army, and finally arrived at the Battery Headquarters.

" We'd almost given you up," I said. " The Major was relieved, wasn't he ? "

" I gathered something like it from his remarks," replied the Hooker with a rueful grin.

" What did he say ? "

" In his own words, as follows : ' Let this be a lesson to you. I hope it has taught you in future to keep in close touch with your infantry. If you'd done so to-night you wouldn't have got into this mess.' D'you know, I felt just like a drunk up at Marlborough Street on the morning after the night before. Can I have a few moments' sleep on your straw ? "

Throughout the night the rumble of the retreating troops along the road continued, punctuated every now and then by the roar of our guns. Dawn broke and the sun rose on our right giving every promise of another scorching day. At 6 a.m. the first elements of the rearguard itself began to pass us, while our weary gunners were having their breakfast of bread-and-meat rissoles brought up to them at the guns in containers, which are large boxes on the thermos-flask principle, that will keep food warm for six hours. The gunners, who had now been firing without cessation for nearly twelve hours, were almost too tired to eat. Dazed with the noise, they continued loading and firing almost automatically, kept on their feet by quarts of strong tea, technically known as " gunfire."

*   *   *   *   *

And at last : " CEASE FIRE. . . ."

Fourteen hours in action without a break. Not a bad baptism. In that time Y–Battery had sent over about sixteen hundred rounds, and Z–Battery, our sister battery on our left, did the same.

All that remained was to pull out as rapidly as possible. Except for M–Troop who, on the far side of the wood in front, still had tricky work to do. They were detailed to stay on for two hours after the rest of us had left, in order to support a battalion of the Guards in the very rear of the rearguard. Then they were to catch us up—if they could. Their prospects of so doing did not look too rosy.

Up came the tractors to the gun positions. The ammunition was packed in the trailers. The guns were taken from the pits, hooked on to the trailers, which in turn were hooked on to the tractors. But the move went slowly. The men were too tired and dazed after the long action to display any alacrity. They were still in the automatic state.

Suddenly, without the slightest warning, a shell burst with an ear-splitting crack just in front of us, a hundred yards in the air. Bullets whizzed in every direction, and a little tight woolly white cloud lingered in the brilliant blue morning sky where the shell had burst.

The Germans had discovered us at last, and were ranging on us with shrapnel.

I take off my hat to shrapnel as a tonic for the jaded. It cracks like the crack of doom—enough to galvanise the dead. It certainly galvanised our deadbeat troops. Weariness dropped from their limbs as by magic. Strength flowed back into tired muscles. Such things as two-hundredweight gun-platforms that, a second before had seemed to weigh tons, and could only be pushed laboriously over the ground by the united efforts of half a dozen gunners, suddenly grew light as feathers, and were tossed up bodily and clamped to the trailers. Mere items such as spades simply flew to their straps on the gun shields almost unassisted. Before the third round of shrapnel had burst the entire column was on the move down the almost empty road, the rearguard having by now practically passed through.

We travelled in silence. Everybody was far too tired to talk. The artificial stimulus administered by the shrapnel soon wore off, and weariness settled on us. A smoke would have helped, but the order in the regiment was : " No smoking in the vehicles." And it was a strict one. Our spirits were not cheered much, moreover, when we thought of M–Troop left behind to take its luck. We knew that the Major himself did not think much of their chances. As we moved off he had been heard to mutter to the Assistant Command Post Officer that we should be damned lucky if we saw them again.

So for about three miles we drove along the main road, holding such conversation as we did hold in monosyllables. And short ones at that. Then, in case the road was shelled by the enemy, we turned off up a lane to the right where bushy trees each side made a passable avenue. Here we halted, and the Major passed a critical eye over the column.

" Well, men," he said tersely, " you've had your first bloody fright. You may smoke."

Whereupon tongues seemed to be released as by a spring. Everyone began swopping experiences. Sleepiness gave place to jokes and laughter. The smoke curled up in the still air from scores of paradisiacal pipes and cigarettes.

And we now headed for our new lines along the Escaut.

II—RED DUST AT OUDENARDE

It was nearly midday when Y–Battery first came in sight of Oudenarde. We arrived just in time. Had we been a few seconds later we should never have seen Oudenarde, even from a distance, as the pretty peaceful little town it was.

This is how it happened.

For the best part of two hours we had been rumbling along in the brilliant spring sunshine along roads and lanes leading westward to the Escaut, on the far side of which, at a place called Wortegem, we anticipated going into action again in support of the British troops defending the passage of the river. That two hours, curiously enough, had been a sort of period of semi-oblivion to us, during which, despite our baptism of battle only just ended, we could easily imagine that no such thing as a war existed. The pleasant, rolling country-side, with its English-style hedges, reminded us of Suffolk. It might have been a bit of agricultural Suffolk with the young crops gladdening the farmer's eye. In the villages, sleepily basking in the thick sun, the inhabitants waved cheerily to us as we passed, completely untroubled, so it seemed, by any pressing fear that in a few hours their homes might be in German hands. You looked to the right and to the left ; and everywhere the picture was of Peace, not War.

And so we began to descend a road that curved round and round the side of a small hill, till at one of the turns Oudenarde appeared, nestling in the dip on the banks of the river, a sweet, ancient-looking medley of grey-tinted walls and red, weathered tiles. It had just those few seconds left to reveal to us, three-quarters of a mile away, its tranquil charm. For its hour had struck. At that very moment between twenty and thirty German bombers swooped down to within a few hundred feet of the roof-tops, and we found ourselves gazing in amazement. For the charming little town had suddenly disappeared and in its place was a cloud of reddish dust and black smoke, here and there pierced by great leaping flames. The swiftness of the attack was staggering, and so was the swiftness of the transfiguration. One minute a town, the next a smudge. Hardly had we begun to hear the thud, thud of the bombs before all was silent. The raiders had vanished, leaving the sky empty again.

And a curious pinkish-red haze marked the spot where Oudenarde had stood ; like a faint blush of shame left hanging in the air by Death and Destruction.

We pushed on towards the wrecked town, possessed by a fearful curiosity. Oudenarde was a ruin. Houses were mere heaps of brick and mortar in most of the streets. There were craters in the roadways that rendered them impassable. Beds had been hurled half-way out of windows, and hung precariously over the pavements. Some of the houses had been neatly sliced in half by the explosion. Pictures still hung on the walls, and ornaments decorated the mantelshelves of the standing half. Curtains flapped mournfully out into the street from windows that had had the sashes entirely ripped away. A reddish dust was settling slowly down on everything. It emanated from the thousands of red roof-tiles the bomb explosions had pulverised. Broken glass carpeted pavements and roads. Our tractors ground it to powder as we passed along.

The inhabitants were still dazed by the fury of the

onslaught.   Rescue work had hardly begun.   Fires were blazing unchecked.   A few women crept out of underground cellars, ghastly grey with terror, sobbing hysterically.   On a grass bank by the river, three little girls, the eldest not more than nine, knelt with the palms of their hands pressed frantically together, praying in front of a wooden Calvary.

It took time to get through the town.   Piles of wreckage and road craters constantly held us up. Finally we arrived at the bridge over the Escaut.   But the bridge was now a ruin of stone and iron.   The German bombers had blown it up just as a column of British infantry was crossing.   Twisted and shattered trucks littered the place, and on the far bank the dead and wounded were still being attended to by their comrades.   Upon them slowly descended the inevitable red dust, like a fine rain of blood.

The Major uttered a very audible curse.

" We'll have to try the bridge higher up the river," he said.   " A nice job it'll be, turning the column round in the middle of this mess.   Get a move on, now. We don't want to be caught here like those fellows were."   He nodded towards the ruins of the bridge.

Now to turn an artillery column a mile long which is jammed in the narrow streets of a town that has been wrecked in an air raid only a few minutes before, beats any jig-saw puzzle ever invented.   You succeed by the combination of much skill, much patience, and much bad language.   And I wouldn't like to assert that the bad language is the least necessary ingredient. Anyhow, before ten minutes had passed bosom friends were unbosoming themselves of pungent (if obscene) criticisms of one another.   Vivid doubts were being cast on the quality of other people's brains with an astounding freedom that passed utterly unnoticed. " Bloody fool " became a compliment by sheer weight of contrast.

In the middle of all the confusion word was passed up from the rear of the column that M-Troop, safe from their hazardous rearguard task, had rejoined the Battery. It will indicate the pressing nature of our present anxiety, with the hum of German bombers overhead again, that, when I shouted the news over to the Major he merely observed : " Oh, very well," though the fate of M-Troop had been on his mind for hours.

After a hot half-hour of unhooking of guns, swinging round, and interminable backing and juggling of tractors, we finally extricated ourselves, and pulled out of ill-fated Oudenarde along a road parallel to the river bank. Five miles down the second bridge was still intact. Over we raced, breathed freely on the other side, took a left turn, and drove forward into the village of Wortegem which had been entirely evacuated. The Battery went into a " hide " underneath over-hanging trees at the side of a road, and the cooks got busy on the midday meal—fried meat-loaf, which can best be described as second cousin to a giant German sausage only without the skin. Bread-crumbs instead. Very friendly when very hungry.

This meal brought us to the ground-floor of our rations, and it was already obvious that in the sort of war that was developing, there might be delay in getting up supplies.

" We'll feed off the land," said the Major. " If we don't have it the Germans will."

So the troops went foraging, and in a short while scores of chickens were on their way to provide the Battery with a stupendous evening meal. Roast chicken and potatoes was to be the menu. We could taste it already !

*   *   *   *   *

It was at this moment that I encountered Boyd, M-Troop Commander, fresh from his rearguard action at Neder Brakel.   A subtle change seemed to have taken place in his appearance.

" Boyd, you look important," I complained.

" Have you ever been cheered by the Guards ? " he asked, mysteriously.

" Has anybody ever been cheered by the Guards ? "

" I have," he said, reverently.

M-Troop had been left behind to support a Guards' battalion, and Boyd had his O.P. near their head-quarters.   Suddenly, marching down the road on the other side of the canal, he beheld a mass of German infantry, nine abreast.   It was a dream-target.   In a matter of seconds he had salvo after salvo crashing into the enemy's ranks.

Now, though the Guards admired the shooting, they showed no enthusiasm towards Boyd.   One of their subalterns came over and said : " We do wish you hadn't done that.   You might have let them come a bit nearer. We were waiting for them with our machine-guns."

Thus Boyd learned that he was considered to have robbed the Guards of one of their legitimate targets. That made him feel a bit sore.

But the position at the Troop post grew so exciting that he soon forgot about it.   The enemy advanced so swiftly that his range dropped to only 1,500 yards, and he expected every minute to find himself firing over open sights.   Ten o'clock arrived, the hour they had orders to quit.   The guns were hitched to the tractors, and they were ready to move off when shells from a German battery showered upon them.   At the same time along the road came the first company of the Guards on the withdrawal.   And they gave the gallant M-Troop a rousing cheer.

" Yes, old fellow, I was cheered by the Guards . . . cheered by the Guards," Boyd concluded in the dreamy voice of a man who has had a glimpse of Paradise.

*   *   *   *   *

It was the Major himself who discovered the butter-factory.   He beckoned me across the main street to a large modern building that hadn't been erected for more than a year.   Inside it was fitted up with a refrigerating plant, and in the warehouse were stacked large wooden cases, all packed with fine fresh butter done up in 2 lb. parcels.

" This'll be useful," said the Major.   " Fresh butter for the Battery is a great thing.   Be sure you have several boxes loaded."

I detailed a party to load seven cases on to a tractor. The news soon spread.   Hardly a man in the Battery failed to make his pilgrimage to the butter-factory, and return with a 2 lb. souvenir packet.   They must have had some trouble with them.   It was over ninety degrees in the shade.

My own great discovery happened shortly after-wards.   The gunners and drivers were getting ready for action again, cleaning the guns, checking sights, filling-up with petrol and oil.   I wandered off round the village, and with no particular reason, entered a cottage in a side-street.   The place had been very thoroughly vacated.   Rooms completely devoid of furniture.   Not even a mat left on the floors.   But opening the door of a room at the back of the house, there *it* stood.   I closed the door stealthily, afraid lest the slightest sound would attract attention from out-side, and with a great idea in my mind, stepped into the street.

It was sheer bad luck that Ritchie, L-Troop's G.P.O., should be standing right outside.   Ritchie in private life is a solicitor.   He possesses to an acute degree the valuable and highly objectionable gift of being able to deduce from the expression on people's faces the thoughts passing through their minds.   He gave me one look and said :

" What have you found inside ? "

" Oh nothing, nothing." I tried to appear entirely unconcerned.

" I'd like to see it, too," he said with a bland smile, and tried to push past me into the house.

I capitulated.

" Ritchie," I said earnestly, " you know as well as I do that there are certain things that one person can enjoy—or even two people ; but if shared among a mob simply benefit nobody."

" I know," he nodded. " The last cigarette in the world."

" Can you keep a secret ? " I continued.

His pained expression was comic. I'd forgotten his civil job. He felt his professional pride wounded.

" Come here," I said, and led him to the back room.

In the centre of the floor stood a large hip-bath. Already the invasion had been on long enough to teach us at least one thing—that hot baths were likely to be highly-rated luxuries in the future.

I explained the idea.

" The essence of a bath is leisure. If the other fellows get to know it's here there'll be a queue, and you and I won't be able to splash in peace. A couple of baths in our own time is the idea. After that I don't care if the whole regiment finds out. What do you say ? "

" All right. On one condition. That I have the first bath."

The cool cheek of this proposition staggered me.

" Be sane," I protested. " Remember, I found it."

" I'm thinking it is more difficult to keep a secret than to find one," he replied, with a glance that filled me with apprehension.

" All right, blackmailer. I agree." I grumbled. " I'll go and tell my servant to bring up some cans of hot water, and towels by the back way. You stay here and don't let a soul enter."

I must say, Ritchie took his time over his bath. I thought he was never coming out. I hung about outside to keep off interlopers. When Ritchie began singing " Johnny was a sailor " at the top of his voice I was terrified.

" Do shut up," I implored. " Somebody will hear and start investigating."

He emerged at last, fresh and clean as new paint. And I remember thinking with satisfaction : " In a few minutes I'll look like that, too."

" Hold the fort for me," I said. " I did for you."

" Certainly, certainly, old fellow," he agreed, with lofty generosity.

I had stripped to the skin and was just about to step into the bath when the door swung open. Ritchie thrust his head in.

" Put on your togs," he cried. " No time for a bath now. Important conference. The Major's waiting for you. Hurry up."

He dashed off.

" Blast ! " I exclaimed. But there was no help for it. I flung on my battledress. The delicious odour of warm soapy water assailed my nostrils like a new torture of Tantalus. " Blast ! " I said again.

The Major sat at the table surrounded by all the other officers when I arrived. And the news was big. He had just returned from the Colonel's conference. We weren't going into action at Wortegem after all. Much to everyone's surprise we were going to leave Belgium and strike south into France. Our immediate destination was Neuve Chapelle.

" Troops must be ready to move in an hour's time," ordered the Major.

And we had eighty chickens on the roast in preparation for a glorious evening's spread !

However, the cooks managed to produce the birds, done to a turn, before we started. But it was a near thing.   We gnawed at our wings and legs, standing by the side of the vehicles, ready to jump in.   Ritchie sauntered up to me, insolently clean.

" You look filthy, old man," he said with a grin. " Why don't you remove some of that grime ?   Have a bath."

I scored a direct hit with a carcase.   But he had given me an idea.

" Run round to that cottage," I said to my servant. " Bring the bath back, and fasten it on to a trailer. And chalk my name on it in case there should be any mistake."

My final deed before moving off was to walk down the column to make sure that my bath hadn't been left behind.   No.   There it was, safely roped on an ammunition trailer, with my name on it in big capitals. And on his own initiative, my servant had inscribed underneath :   " Private and Personal."

III—Southward to Arras

We crossed the frontier at Halluin, near Menin, having avoided all the main roads, and followed the bank of the Lys through Comines to Armentières. It was midnight, and the town was silent and deserted. Most of us fell to sentimental thinking of happy times during our four months in billets here. Going up the Rue de Sadi-Carnot, I passed my own billet—billet of a lifetime—the palatial mansion of M. Guillaume, the wealthy mill-owner. Not a sign of life there now. Every window shuttered. And these people who had been so kind to me during my long illness—what had happened to them in the three short weeks since I said goodbye ? Had they passed out of my life for ever ? Jovial M. Guillaume, with his hearty laugh, who used to sip his liqueur and coffee after dinner at my bedside. His pretty wife who whiled away my dreary afternoons chatting to me in her amusing broken English. And blonde, vivacious, intelligent, six-year-old Jeannette who, when I was up and about, insisted that I and no other should take her to school in the mornings. We walked along hand-in-hand. And I fancy she liked to parade me in front of her schoolfellows. She was a terrible little flirt, and I shouldn't be surprised if she told them she was in love with me. And I with her !

And now, all I could do was to hope the War would deal kindly with them.

On through Laventie to Neuve Chapelle, where we arrived as dawn was breaking. Here we expected to remain for a day. A farmhouse was allotted to the troops, a mess was set up in another farm, and we promised ourselves sleep, much of it, for the first time in forty-eight hours. As we entered Neuve Chapelle, the inhabitants departed, great farm-carts piled high with their belongings. What they could not take they bequeathed to us.

"Monsieur le Capitaine," said an old farmer who met me in the street, "there are three fine pigs in my farm down the road there. Will you eat them ? "

I promised to do my best, with a little assistance.

We had just finished breakfast when the Major hurried into the mess.

"Be ready to move in half an hour," he said. "We're going on to Vimy. We may be in action there."

Once more the guns were hooked in, and once more we took the road, through Lens, murky and depressing despite the bright day, and south towards Vimy. Now we got caught in a new flood of refugees, French this time, fleeing north from Arras and the surrounding districts with the one hope of getting to the Channel ports. The same heartrending procession, on wheels and on foot. Often the pedestrians carried just one red blanket, rolled, and tied bandolier-fashion over the shoulder. All they had been able to save of their worldly possessions. One blanket to wrap themselves in at night. The women, from the point of view of attire, presented a striking contrast. Some were clothed entirely on principle of utility—stout, low-heeled shoes, waterproofs, and berets, or handkerchiefs swathed round their heads. Others had not possessed strength to make the great sacrifice. They struggled along in smart hats, fur coats, and the daintiest of footwear, some even stopping for a moment to consult their vanity mirrors to see how their make-up was faring under its supreme test. The eternal, unquenchable, feminine !

Thousands and thousands and thousands of refugees, all pressing in one direction, driven on by ceaseless terror, without order and without control. And struggling to force a passage in the opposite direction through this panic-stricken army were all the machines of war, British and French, tanks, guns, mortars, companies of mitrailleuses with motor cycles, their heavy machine-guns carried in side-cars, and trucks upon trucks of infantry. The confusion and shouting and screaming and cursing was a war in itself. Often a farm-cart would decide to pull out and try to pass the vehicle in front. Then the entire military column was held up till the chaos died down a bit. That sometimes took half an hour. This in a speed-war when every minute was precious, and an obstreperous farm-cart might lose us a lump of France !

*   *   *   *   *

It took us half a day to reach Vimy, a distance of ten miles.

I was leading the Battery through the middle of this chaos when a junior Staff officer stepped off the kerb.

" Are you the 2004th Field Regiment ? " he asked.

" Yes."

" D'you know where your Colonel is ? "

I told him the Colonel had gone forward with the Major on a reconnaissance.

" I'm Second-in-Command of the Battery. Can I do anything ? "

" Will you come along and see the Brigadier ? "

I sent the Battery on to a rendezvous near Givenchy, and the Staff officer drove me in his car up the Lens-Arras road towards the Vimy Ridge. At the cross roads just this side of the ridge, the Brigadier sat on the ground, his back against the wall of a house.

" You'll have to take the orders," he said, when I explained the Colonel's absence. " You must go into action immediately. Give me your map."

He marked the O.P. area, which was the eastern half of the ridge, and the battery areas, just behind the ridge on the long side. At that moment the Colonel arrived. After a brief conversation the two of us drove off to Givenchy and squatted on the pavement against the church tower waiting for the Troop Commanders to come up to give them orders for deployment.

*   *   *   *   *

It was nearly four in the afternoon when I put my head over the top of Vimy Ridge for the first time, and gazed on the battle in the distance. To the left lay Arras, in the middle distance of the plain, but a thick curtain of smoke hung before it. A bombing attack was in progress, and the heavy explosions punctuated the continual distant thunder of the gunfire. Now and again the sound of sharp vicious bursts of machine-gun fire mingled with the heavier boom. Beyond this incessant rumble of storm, no sign of war marred the level landscape that stretched far away to where the cone of Mont St. Eloi rose on the right, a landscape green, unscarred, serene, studded with pretty red villages, and clumps of thick woods, very much like the Kentish Weald, except for the straight lines of tall poplars marking the roads.

With the help of my O.P. Ack, my telephone operator, and one spade I excavated a hole on the Lens side of the ridge in which I could stand and observe, only my head projecting over the top. A couple of wires were laid to the guns in case one was broken by enemy shell-fire. At any moment now orders to shell the enemy might be expected. But the hours went by and they never came. Yonder at Arras the

Welsh Guards, with a rock-like defence, were stemming, for the time being, the central advance.

Night fell, and on the screen of the darkness along the horizon the battle became more visible. The whole front lit up with red flashes of bursting bombs and shells. Two big fires were blazing and the glare coloured the sky a dirty pink. One bomb had evidently found a petrol store, and the flames were ascending in great rolling billows. High in the sky, above all this, an incredible fire-work display went on for hours. Tracer shells made weird and wonderful designs in fiery orange loops. Now and again up shot a rocket which burst into a ball of brilliant coloured light that shone for a few seconds and vanished. Less frequently, Very Lights burst, either red, green, blue or yellow, which floated about for a full half-minute before expiring. As a spectacle it was tremendous.

An artillery observer does more than direct fire. Part of his job is to report back at once anything unusual that he sees or hears in his zone. This information goes to Regimental Headquarters, is sifted and sent on to Division, where it is again sifted and studied and collated with similar information sent from other sources. Thus much valuable knowledge is obtained.

The battle round Arras gave me a busy time, what with its conflagrations, sudden bursts of machine-gun fire in unexpected directions, and its fireworks. Up soared a yellow rocket.

" Get me the A.C.P.O." I say to my telephone operator . . . .

" Hello . . . Another piece of nonsense for you. Just seen a yellow rocket go up. Bearing 210°. About six miles away. Time, 23.30 hours (11.30 p.m.)."

And so it went on, while the chill nip in the night

113   H

air on the exposed Ridge caused me to wrap my great-coat tighter round me.

I remember thinking our people seemed to be doing very well over there in front. No S.O.S. (red-over-green-over-red) signals, and very few white Very Lights. Which showed that the infantry weren't jittery.

Suddenly, up soared a rocket far in front of me. that burst into a white ball. A German success rocket. The indication to their Headquarters that an objective (some village or wood) had been captured. Shortly after, two more to the left of Arras, and then others over to the right.

At slow intervals, hour by hour, the white rockets continued to burst in the sky to my left, creeping round and round till in the darkness they seemed at last to be coming up from over my left shoulder.

Of course they were a long way away, though in the darkness they appeared close. But alone in the middle of the night on the top of Vimy Ridge, watching those white balls steadily advancing in the sky, gave me a queer sensation. I wasn't sorry when dawn broke and the Babe came along to relieve me.

" Damn cold, isn't it ? " he said, and pretending abysmal ignorance added : " What do you do on these occasions ? "

" You have a nice sleep," I replied. " And someone brings you up a cup of tea in the morning, and a copy of *The Times*. And it won't be me."

The Major was reclining on his camp bed when I returned to the Command Post.

" I should call it a day," he said. " Get some sleep."

I thought so, too. On top of the long journey from Belgium I had done over twelve hours on the Ridge.

Rolling my blankets round me, I fell fast asleep on the floor.

IV—Liaison with the Infantry

The faint sound of voices murmuring at the far end
of a mile-long tunnel grew louder and louder till they
drummed my ear. I awoke. It was the Major in
conversation with the Troop Commanders and the
Command Post Officer. I glanced at my watch.
Half-past nine. Five hours of a dream sleep had been
mine.

Seeing the Command Post displaying distinct signs
of activity made me a bit self-conscious of my horizontal ease. So I rolled out of my blanket.

Much to my surprise the Major said :

" You needn't be in a hurry to get up. You
won't be going to the O.P. I've a special job for
you."

" Not one I can do in bed by any chance, sir," I
exclaimed. " What a fine war this is."

He laughed and went out with the Troop Commanders. I started to dress, eating my boiled eggs
off the mantelpiece.

" What's moving ? " I asked the C.P.O., who looked
busy.

" We are," he drawled, in his soft composed voice.
" We're going to take part in the attack south-west
of Arras with the M—th Division."

" Sounds big business. When do we start ? "

" In an hour."

" Then I'll have another egg. I always eat more
standing up."

The Germans were pressing forward westward
through a corridor about twenty miles across, just

below Arras. A big attempt was being made to close the corridor. The French were to attack from the south, while the British struck down to join them from west of Arras. Y-Battery formed part of one of the two composite mobile columns engaged in the counter-attack.

At half-past ten the Battery pulled out of positions and took the Lens-Arras road over the left side of Vimy Ridge towards Arras. At the village of Ecurie, a mile and a half from Arras, we branched off to the right. In front we could hear the bursting shells and bombs, the rattle of machine-guns, and scattered rifle fire, where the grim struggle for Arras was raging. Over Arras itself hung a thick pall of smoke, very distinct and sombre against the wide sweep of the sky's otherwise flawless blue.

The Major had proceeded ahead with the infantry commander, taking along our Wagon-Lines officer whose job it was to find us a " hide " in the vicinity of the village of Anzin St. Aubin. Here the Battery was to meet him. This morning the main road was surprisingly clear of fugitives. The flood had exhausted itself at last, and the troops could now move forward unhampered. A regiment of French cuirassiers (mechanised, with four-seater cars, and motorcycle combinations carrying machine-guns) were halted by the roadside, and on the outskirts of a ruined village a British motor-cycle machine-gun battalion was waiting to go into action.

We climbed a small rise into Anzin St. Aubin where the Wagon-Lines Officer met us. His honest face was aglow with enthusiasm. He had (he said) found us the ideal " hide " You could tell that he felt inwardly positive there wasn't another such " hide " to be found in the whole of France. Proudly he led us into the grounds of a deserted château encircled by a broad drive, tree-lined on both sides. On the face of it there seemed every reason to agree with the Wagon-Lines Officer   All we had to do was to drive through the main gates and circle round the wide path.   In a few minutes our vehicles were coiled serpent-wise round the château, concealed by the trees.

The place had evidently only recently been vacated. The wide lawn in front of the house was close-cropped. Flower beds were blooming and tidy.   The white wooden seats on the lawn glistened in the sunshine with their new paint.   It made a very pretty picture. But the picture would have been much prettier if we hadn't seen three unmistakable shell-holes on the lawn.   They were as ominous as Man Friday's footprints.

" All I can say is I hope they don't start to hot it up again," I said to the Wagon-Lines Officer, cheerfully.   The cooks began preparing the midday meal, and the men obeyed orders to get as much sleep as possible.

I walked over to my truck.   " Get in touch with the Major," I said to the wireless operator.

He adjusted the ear-phones, held the microphone in front of his lips, and began his sing-song chant.

" Robert Eddy calling X . . . Robert Eddy calling X . . . can you hear me ? can you hear me ? . . . if so answer . . ."

(Robert Eddy (for R.E.) identified my truck and X was the Major's tactical sign.)

Then he switched over to receiving and after a second or two came the reply :

" X calling Robert Eddy . . . X calling Robert Eddy . . . I can hear you . . . I can hear you . . . strength sevener . . . remain on receive . . . remain on receive . . . over to you over . . ."

(Strength sevener, meant he was hearing well. Over to you over, meant it was the other's turn to transmit.)

Back my operator switched to transmission.

"Robert Eddy calling X . . . Robert Eddy calling X . . . I have received message . . . I have received message . . . over to you over . . ."

Having established contact and left my wireless ready to receive orders at once from the Major, I departed to lunch off bully beef, hot potatoes, and the inevitable tea.

We had finished the meal, and were basking in the glorious sunshine when, with a loud prolonged swish-sh-sh-sh a shell tore through the air just over our heads and burst in a field a hundred yards away.

"The ideal 'hide,'" laughed Tops, N–Troop Commander. "Evidently being followed by the ideal 'seek.'"

And in rapid succession a dozen more shells swished over our heads, all bursting in the same field. Then we had peace again. But I hoped we should soon be on the move. This château looked too much like a registered target to be comfortable.

Half an hour later there was a commotion at the main gate of the château. I walked over to see what the trouble was. Our sentry had planted himself very determinedly in the centre of the drive, with his left hand extended like a traffic policeman in Piccadilly Circus. Outside the gate was the same regiment of cuirassiers we had passed earlier in the day.

"They want to pinch our ' 'ide,' sir," explained the sentry, indignantly.

Now there is much jealousy over good "hides." When you find one you don't welcome interlopers. For this important reason : that while you yourself may have got there without being observed, you have no guarantee the arrival of the newcomers may likewise have passed unnoticed, and that you may not get an undeserved share of the unwelcome attentions they have attracted. Hence the sentry's indignation.

I had a word with the French commander, explained the château's apparent lure for enemy shells, and told him he was very welcome to make what use of the place he wished. As he was thanking me politely a gunner ran up.

" You're wanted at the set, sir," he said.

I hurried to the truck, fixed on the ear-phones, and held the microphone to my lips.

" Captain —— speaking . . . Captain —— speaking . . . ready to receive your message . . . ready to receive your message . . . over to you over . . ."

" We're going into action " came the Major's voice. " I want you, the C.P.O. and his assistant, and the Gun Position Officers to meet me without delay at the first cross-roads at Dainville. Gun groups will remain in their present ' hide.' Got it ? "

I repeated back, dashed out of the truck and shouted " Orders ! " The other officers and the senior sergeants gathered round and we studied the maps.

" Any questions ? " I asked. " No ? Then off we go."

At the cross-roads the Major emerged from a wayside barn looking rather shaken up.

" Anything wrong, sir ? " I asked.

" I've just had the shave of my life," he replied. " Come in the barn and I'll show you."

Certainly it was a shave to be proud of. Just as the Major had reached the village the enemy started to shell it violently. He took cover in the barn and a shell exploded dead on the roof, bowling him over. As he went down something whizzed right past his ear.

" And here it is," he added, reverently producing from his pocket the nose of a shell. " It was so hot when I picked it up that it burned my hand."

I touched that shell nose for luck a minute later

when I found I had been detailed to do liaison with the front-line infantry in the impending action.

" The 7th Battalion of the Blankshires are in front," said the Major. " Get off to their Battalion Head-quarters. You'll probably find them somewhere on the road towards Achicourt."

I jumped into my truck, and accompanied by my wireless operator and driver, started off in the direction of Achicourt, about two miles south of Arras. Our infantry were advancing very rapidly just now. We travelled through country still occupied by small detachments of Germans who had been cut off. Mopping-up parties of Tommies were investigating the farmhouses, and occasionally bringing out a few prisoners. Every now and then a little spasmodic shooting indicated that resistance was still being offered.

Everywhere there were signs of fierce shelling and bombing. At a small hamlet just outside Achicourt my truck was held up by a huge crater where a bomb had dropped plumb in the centre of the road. Troops were busy filling in the hole before traffic could pass The hamlet itself was a heap of ruins. Suddenly round the corner of the road, marching in fours, appeared a column of German infantry. Prisoners. A Tommy with fixed bayonet marched in front. There were about four hundred of them, a good bag for the Blankshires. They were a fine-looking lot of fellows, bronzed, fair-haired, clean shaven—in fact so fresh and clean-looking that they couldn't have done much fighting. Probably they had been brought right up to the front line in vehicles and captured almost immediately they alighted. The bulk of them were between twenty-five and thirty, and they looked so smart in their slate-blue uniforms, their blue helmets with the gold eagle on the side, and their new black jack-boots, that they suggested the parade ground rather than the battle-field. They were headed by a short, weedy-looking

German officer with a face like Goebbels. He strode along in an arrogant swagger, and was a bit of a blemish on the otherwise satisfactory procession.

The crater being now filled in, I went forward in my search for the Battalion Headquarters, stopping every now and then to ask an officer or sergeant for information. The answer was always the same : " Further on." Evidently the infantry was still going forward. I reached Achicourt, which had suffered heavily from shell-fire, and still there was no sign of the front line. Except for stray parties of troops, and a couple of ambulances into which stretcher parties were unloading casualties, the village was deserted.

We left Achicourt behind and drove along down a road devoid of traffic. Here and there on the grass verge infantry soldiers who had been wounded in the day's advance were having their injuries dressed by R.A.M.C. men. It was now late in the afternoon, but the sun, beating from a cloudless sky, was as hot as at noon. We crossed a railway bridge, and then the road led dead straight to the village of Beaurains through open country, with fields on either side where a number of British and French tanks were being overhauled by their crews.

And at last, by the cross-roads just outside Beaurains, I found Battalion Headquarters. In a ditch, of all places.

A reserve line of infantry was lying in this long shallow ditch for a mile along the roadside, and with them their Colonel and his Second-in-Command.

" Good afternoon, sir," I said, introducing myself. " I'm gunner liaison officer."

" Welcome, my boy," exclaimed the Colonel heartily. " Take a seat in the ditch. Is your battery ready to fire ? "

" Give us a quarter of an hour. What targets would you like us to fire on ? "

We scanned our maps for likely enemy concentration points, deciding on four villages along the banks of the River Cojeul, about four miles distant.

"Those villages are our final objective," said the Colonel. "The enemy will probably try to bring his infantry over the bridges. Anyhow, they're good targets to have a crack at to begin with. Have you any means of communication with your battery?"

Unfortunately I hadn't. I had followed up the infantry so far that I had exceeded the range of my wireless.

"I'll return to the Battery, give them the targets, send up an O.P. officer, and have a telephone line laid direct to you," I said.

"Look out," suddenly shouted the Colonel. "Cover your map up. Those damn things show up for miles."

Thirty German bombers appeared over our heads. We lay flat in the ditch with our faces to the ground, lest these, too, might be visible.

The planes passed over without paying us any attention. As soon as they were gone I returned to my truck and set off back to the Battery.

Near Dainville, about a mile and a half from the area that was to be occupied by our battery position, two French tanks were drawn up stationary on the road alongside a small copse. As I approached, five Messerschmitts wheeled around, one behind the other, in preparation to attack them. The tanks had also seen the planes, and were just closing their turrets. I guessed what was coming their way, and hoped to get past in time to avoid getting a share of it. But I was too late. Just as I came abreast of the tanks the first plane was beginning its dive right overhead.

"Jump for it," I yelled. I shot out of one side of the truck as my driver and wireless operator took a headlong leap out of the other. I scrambled into a hedgeless ditch by the roadside just as the German machine-guns began to spray the road. My ditch was so shallow that I could only partly conceal my head. Bullets whizzed in front of my face. When they smacked the dry earth at the edge of the ditch puffs of dust spurted up, half blinding me. Every now and then a bullet flew so close that the blast hit me in the face like a punch, and I touched myself to see if I had been wounded, and was quite surprised not to find blood on my hand. For nearly ten minutes the fight went on, the planes circling round a hundred feet up and the tanks firing back at them. When silence came I poked my head up gingerly out of the ditch.

"Williams! Simson! Are you all right?" I called to my two men.

"Yes, sir," came back the welcome answer in muffled tones. But there was no sign of them anywhere.

Shaking the dust out of my eyes and ears, I walked back to my truck. Williams and Simson suddenly wriggled out on their bellies like eels from underneath one of the tanks. They had crawled in between the tracks with only a foot of space to do it in.

"Suppose the tank had moved on?" I said, with a shudder.

"We didn't have time to think about it, sir."

Anyhow, we couldn't show a scratch between us, and when we came to examine the truck we realised our luck. It was riddled with bullets. In the splinter-proof glass of the windscreen there were thirteen holes in front of my seat. The bullets had passed right through the back of the seat into the wireless operator's kit.

When we reached the Battery Command Post my truck became an exhibition. Everybody came along to inspect it. The Major's narrow shave of the morning receded into the background of ancient history. My perforated windscreen put his shell-nose right out of joint. I decided on the spot to make a mascot of that windscreen, and to stick to it as long as the War lasted. So impressed was I, indeed, by it, that I even toyed with the idea of taking it back to England with me on my next leave. It was the first sign of my surrender to the Great Goddess Luck, who, once a war gets going, isn't long before she gathers in her converts by the thousand.

*　　　*　　　*　　　*　　　*

" I've got some targets," I said to the Major, and explained the infantry's need of us. " Harassing fire tasks."

And the Command Post Officer settled down to work them out from my map.

Boyd, M–Troop commander, whom the Major had selected as the forward O.P. officer, came up to me before leaving for a chat about possibilities.

" Our forward line is in front of Beaurains," I said, " and I don't think you'll do better for an O.P. than the village church. You should get a pretty view from the belfry."

" I love sightseeing," he said with a grin, and hurried ' off with his O.P.Ack, telephonist and wireless operator. Behind followed a cable-laying truck with half a dozen signallers, and the N.C.O. in charge on a motor-cycle.

We were now awaiting the arrival of the guns from the " hide " at Anzin St. Aubin. The gun positions had already been marked out by the Gun Position Officers. They were about half a mile away from the Battery Command Post, which had been set up in the caretaker's house of a brick factory. N–Troop was in the far corner or the brick-field, M–Troop was under an embankment, and L–Troop were at the corner of a hedge in another field.

Suddenly, as we stood looking down the road, over

a hundred bombers roared in the sky and began to bomb Dainville (which was already under shell fire) and its surroundings. The thunder of the explosions was terrific. Huge clouds of smoke and dust swirled in the air, a score of fires were started, and the whole village was blotted out from our view by a solid pall, behind which it didn't take much imagination to guess the horrors that were happening.

And at this very moment, where on the far side the road curved down to the village, we saw the long line of Y–Battery vehicles driving straight into this inferno. Now a battery going into action stops for nothing. Before we had time to gasp they had disappeared, swallowed up in the deadly chaos that was going on behind that dark curtain.

" My God ! " exclaimed the Major aghast. " That's the last of them ! "

No one else spoke. He had said all there was to say.

*   *   *   *   *

Battle in the new style has this advantage. It leaves you no time to dwell upon your thoughts. Events succeed one another so swiftly that before you have settled down to brood upon one set of emotions an entirely different one is set in train. So it was now. Nine dive-bombers had their attention attracted to us by a truck which had been inadvertently left standing on the road. We saw them coming at us in flights of three. They circled round overhead and on the second circle formed in line to make their dive. We saw the leader do a half-roll and dive, so it seemed, straight at us, with a nerve-shattering scream that rose to a crescendo the nearer he came. At about five hundred feet from the ground, three bombs, like a clutch of black ostrich eggs, dropped from the plane. They also seemed to be coming straight for us.

We stopped to see no more. In fact, we hadn't

really waited to see anything. A wild rush began
for the cellar of the Command Post. The Major and
I had the farthest to run, and he was a few yards in
front of me. Racing along by the side of a brick wall,
I saw the Major hurl himself through the doorway,
gather a couple of people who stood at the top of the
stairs in a flying tackle, and crash into the cellar in a
heap. I had still four yards to go and knew now that
I couldn't hope to beat the bomb. So I flung myself
forward flat on the ground as far as I could reach.
And just as I did so the first bomb exploded. The
blast catching me in the rear, very forcibly propelled
me over the remaining distance, head-first through
the cellar doorway. But here was no haven. There
wasn't even standing room. I turned to seek cover
in a room at the side on the ground level. Then the
second bomb burst and this time the blast blew me
headlong through the swing-door of the room into
what felt like a quicksand, wherein I slowly sank and
sank. When I could extricate my head, I was half
suffocated. I had been hurled into a roomful of loose
corn, which covered the floor four feet deep. There
I stayed, my head sticking up out of the corn, while
the bombs continued to burst outside. Each explosion
shook the house on its foundations and filled the air
with the noise of crashing glass. Then came the usual
" raid over " silence, and I waded out of the corn as
white as a miller from head to foot.

Outside the truck that had caused the trouble had
had all its tyres punctured.

*   *   *   *   *

Again we had no time to dwell on our experiences.
A fresh emotion was ready to grip us. Glancing up
the road, to our joy and amazement we beheld the
leading gun-tractor of Y-Battery just emerging from

the smoke and conflagration and tumult of Dainville. And behind it another tractor. And another.

We stood there counting them aloud as they rumbled out of that dreadful holocaust in which we had feared they were lost for ever.

One. . . . Two. . . . Three. . . . Four. . . . Five. . . ." The whole twelve of them. Not one lost.

" A miracle," breathed the Major fervently.

And once more we considered he had said it all.

M- and L-Troops deployed to their positions before they reached us. N-Troop had to pass the Command Post to get to theirs. When we saw the savage expression on the usually serene and smiling countenance of Tops, the Troop Commander, we felt a little uneasy. Perhaps something had gone amiss.

Something had. As the Troop Commander passed us he shouted angrily from his truck :

" Sergeant Barber killed."

The sergeant had been hit in the face by a shell splinter when coming through Dainville, and killed instantaneously.

He was our first casualty. A first-rate sergeant and a fine No. 1 on the gun. His death wrought a subtle change throughout the Battery. We had looked on many dead and dying in the last days. For instance, there was the infantry at the bridge at Oudenarde. But as is the case in war, you soon learn to witness such things from a detached point of view. Until something that touches you more personally happens. Then the attitude changes.

So it was henceforth with Y-Battery. I suppose it was because we now had something of our own to avenge.

V—THE TANKS BREAK THROUGH

Twilight was falling when, for the second time that day, I departed for the infantry line to resume liaison. Y-Battery's guns were already in action, shelling the bridges over the Cojeul that the Colonel had selected. At Achicourt, outside a house where a lot of German wounded were being attended to by our troops, I inquired of a Blankshire sergeant if Battalion Headquarters had moved. After the speed with which our infantry had advanced earlier in the day, I was fully prepared to embark on another long chase.

But the Colonel was still in the ditch at the crossroads. The change that had taken place in the situation was not the one I expected. Shadowy figures of men, in ones, twos and threes, were moving over the darkening fields towards us. They ran forward, crouching as they came. In the gloom I took them for Germans, and a thrill ran through me at stepping right into the middle of an attack. At any moment I expected to hear the crackle of our infantry fire from the waiting troops in the ditch. I crouched down by the Colonel in the ditch.

" Germans ? " I asked, trying to speak coolly.

" No, damn it," he replied. " That's our front line coming back. We've withdrawn from Beaurains."

My thoughts immediately flew to Boyd, stuck up there in the belfry of the church I had recommended.

" I've an O.P. officer in Beaurains," I said. " Has he been warned ? "

" Your O.P. went back some time ago, I think," the Colonel answered.

" Oh no. He went forward again," remarked the Second in Command.

I stopped to hear no more. A vivid picture presented itself of Boyd in the belfry, blissfully ignorant of the infantry's withdrawal, suddenly finding himself hauled out by Germans.

" Drive like hell to Beaurains," I told the driver, looking to see that my revolver was loaded. We covered the distance, about a thousand yards, in no time. The shell-marked village was deadly silent. Not a sound in the streets, not a soul to be seen, British or German. Its unnatural hush and utter emptiness produced a queer effect in the deepening twilight. Much too quiet to be good. Swinging round a corner on two wheels, I came across our cable party busily engaged laying the wire back to the Battery, and utterly oblivious of their peril.

" Cut the wire and get back to the cross roads," I yelled, without stopping.

Boyd's truck was standing outside the church. " Get that engine running at once," I shouted to his driver, and dashed into the building.

Inside there was almost complete darkness. I pitched over a stool, picked myself up, and ran up and down the side aisles opening all the little doors I could see to discover which led to the belfry. Finally through one of them I dimly saw a winding staircase.

" Boyd, Boyd," I shouted up.

No reply, except a magnificent echo.

Still calling, I commenced to grope up the dark staircase. At last he heard me.

" Hello, hello," he answered in his best unperturbed manner. " What's all the fuss ? War over ? "

" It will be for you if you don't come down damn quick," I shouted back. " The Germans are entering the village. Bring the telephone and cut the wire."

He was down those stairs with his two assistants in

a matter of seconds. We jumped pell-mell into our trucks.

" Here they come," I said, and there sounded a heavy rumble of the German tanks entering the other end of the village.

A rocket whizzed up over our heads high into the night sky and burst into a white ball. It was a German " success rocket," indicating to their headquarters that Beaurains had been taken.

We'd got out with nothing to spare.

*   *   *   *   *

Back at the cross-roads, Boyd and I held a hurried conference about establishing a new O.P., and it was decided he should prospect for one between the infantry front line and Achicourt. I returned to the ditch to resume my liaison. The infantry were still lining the road, but Battalion Headquarters had moved back down the road towards Achicourt. Nobody could say exactly where. Again I began hunting them, this time in the darkness, the moon not having risen yet. At Achicourt a sergeant-major informed me that Battalion Headquarters had left five minutes ago. He thought they'd gone up in the Beaurains direction. So back I went, asking questions and getting nowhere. Then I thought I'd try the other side of Achicourt towards Dainville. No luck. And I headed back once more to Achicourt.

I hadn't proceeded far before meeting signs that an entirely new situation had arisen. Towards me, down the road from Achicourt struggled little batches of our infantry, dust-stained, grimy, some without their tin helmets and rifles, and all struggling along under a dead-weight of weariness. They displayed all the signs of a rough time. Stopping a corporal I asked what had happened.

" The bloody tanks have smashed through us," he

said fiercely. " We've had to withdraw. The bastards
are chasing us now."

There appeared something wrong about this. True,
not long before I had seen the German tanks enter
Beaurains ; but that was well on the other side of
Achicourt. I felt sure there must be some exaggeration. The corporal vanished into a field and I drove
forward, dodging the driblets of retiring infantry
hastening in the other direction. After a while they
thinned out and the road became bare.

" Bloke seemed a bit worried, sir," observed my
driver casually, and we negotiated a bend.

My heart gave a sudden bound and seemed to get
stuck in my throat. Not more than three hundred
yards in front, its nose pointing towards us, a stationary
German tank blocked the road.

" Quick ; turn her round," I gasped. But the
driver wanted no telling. He swung the car over so
abruptly that the wheels almost left the ground.

It was now a case of getting back to the Battery at
top speed to warn them of their danger. We had two
miles to go and we wasted no time. Many of the weary
infantry tried to stop us for a lift. I was more than sorry
for them, but I dared not do it. I'd have immediately
been overloaded, and never reached my destination.

As it was, with still a mile to go, the car suddenly
stopped, although the engine continued to run all
right. We put it in gear ; but not a budge. That
swift turn had done the damage. There was nothing
else but to abandon it, and with it my riddled windscreen mascot that I had flattered myself I was going
to stick to throughout the war. Instead of which
here was I forced to part with it after being under its
protection for a mere six hours. A pity. No denying
it had been doing its job well.

Having smashed the wireless set, we started to foot
it across the fields in the direction in which the Battery

lay. They were still firing at the original targets,
ignorant of what had happened in the past couple of
hours to the front line. After a while we emerged
by the hedge in front of L–Troop's guns, and I went
forward in the darkness shouting my name at the top
of my voice in case the Bren gunner might make a
mistake and start some practice.

I found the Major outside the Command Post, leaning against the wall, smoking a cigarette and chatting
leisurely with the A.C.P.O. Not having been chasing
Battalion Headquarters over the country on and off
for hours, he had been able to enjoy a comfortable
meal and was feeling quite happy with himself. My
sudden appearance, breathless, made him stare.

" We're in a hot spot, sir," I said. " Enemy tanks
are only a mile or so away. They may be nearer now.
There's no infantry in front of us. We're in grave danger
of being cut off. God knows what's happened to Boyd."

I followed with a swift account of what I'd seen.

" I can't believe it," he said.

" It's true," I insisted.

" It can't be," he said, quite peremptorily.

His manner began to irritate me. He seemed to
be informing me I was a liar. It was only another
step for me to imagine he thought I was panicking.

" Come up the road and see for yourself," I said.
" We won't have far to go."

Still he was not convinced. Again I told him I'd
seen the tank with my own eyes.

" Who told you about the infantry retiring ? A
responsible officer ? "

" It was a very expressive corporal. He seemed to
know what he was talking about."

In the heat of the moment I quite overlooked the
fact that I had been just as incredulous at first of the
corporal as the Major now was of me. A little personal
conviction makes a lot of difference on such occasions.

" I can't take the responsibility," said the Major firmly. " Take my truck. Go back and see if you can find some responsible officer. The Battery continues in action."

Although ruffled by the doubts the Major had cast on my information, I admired the coolness with which he faced a difficult situation. Off I tore up the road again in his truck till I once more encountered the straggling infantry. The nearest approach to a " responsible officer " I could discover was a dog-tired young subaltern who could hardly keep his eyes open as he stumbled along the road. His statement verified and amplified the corporal's. The Germans, he said, had delivered a terrific counter-attack to the south-west of Arras with hundreds of tanks. Our infantry had been outflanked on the right and attacked in the rear. The British tanks had come up against the huge German thirty-five-ton tanks for the first time, and suffered heavy casualties. Achicourt had been outflanked, too, and the enemy was still pushing forward.

Back to the Major I sped with the subaltern's information. That clinched it. Orders were given to cease fire, and the Battery prepared in haste to pull out. The Major and I stayed behind till the last tractor had vanished.

" Look ! " I exclaimed, pointing up the road leading from the south-west. The shadowy shapes of half a dozen German tanks were visible, slowly crawling our way.

We jumped into the truck and took a short cut across fields to meet the Battery lower down the road.

" Well, you were right after all," said the Major with a smile. " I'm sorry if I seemed to doubt you. But it wanted a bit of believing. No hard feelings, eh ? "

In face of the triumphant confirmation so kindly provided on my behalf by the six German tanks, I could afford to be generous.

133

VI—Horror by moonlight

We didn't know it at the time, but when Y-Battery pulled out that night, almost in the shadow of the German tanks, there began for us the long, long retreat that was only to end on the bloodstained beaches of Dunkirk. The attempt to seal up the corridor south of Arras had failed, and our part in that operation was over. Never again in the harried days to follow were we destined to move forward. Northward we zig-zagged with the remainder of our stubborn troops over a hundred and fifty arduous miles separating us from the sea, fighting by day and moving under cover of night. Rarely were we to be in action again for more than a day in the same place. Move, move, move, all the time. As N–Troop Commander remarked on one occasion: " Talk about caravanning. . . ."

*   *   *   *   *

When the Major and I overtook the Battery the road was pretty crowded with our retreating infantry. Back at Anzin St. Aubin a halt was ordered while we checked up on the tractors. All correct, despite our abrupt departure. The Major departed to endeavour to find the Colonel, last heard of at Regimental H.Q. at Marœuil, some five miles off. I took the Battery along to re-occupy our old positions on Vimy Ridge. Through Neuville St. Vaast we proceeded over the Ridge to Givenchy and turned right to Vimy, where I halted the Battery and went forward a mile to reconnoitre the gun positions. The sight that greeted me turned my blood cold. Heaps of dead and dying men, women and children filled our gun-pits. They were refugees who had taken cover there, and been literally blasted out of life some hours earlier by German bombers, probably looking for us. From the interior of these piles of torn, limbless, decapitated bodies sounded an occasional groan where some un-fortunate still drew breath. A sickening stench per-vaded the warm air. Upon this spectacle of horror the midnight moon shone brightly from a cloudless sky.

My driver and I stared at each other speechless. Our feelings were beyond words. The total absence of any sign that these poor wretches had received any assistance accentuated the horror. The mangled piles remained, after all these hours, in exactly the same state as when the bombers had finished with them. No succour, no relief, no medical attention of any sort. Even the dead had been left to choke, with the weight of their bodies, the last breath out of the injured. It was typical of the utter breakdown of the French civilian relief services all over the northern invasion area. Perhaps such services had never even been in existence outside the few biggest towns. Certainly there was never a hint of refugee camps, mobile canteens, or civilian casualty stations. As for anything resembling our own A.R.P. . . .

The miserable refugees received no instructions where to make for. There was never a gendarme to be seen controlling and directing them. They just wandered along in a dumb panic, bombed here, machine-gunned there, imploring any troops they met to tell them a safe route to take to get away from the Germans. To proffer advice on such occasions was dubious assist-ance. So quickly did the situation change that it was quite easy, without knowing it, to shepherd inquirers straight towards the German tanks.

From these ghastly gun-pits I drove over to what

had been the Battery Command Post. Here another nightmare. The entire front of the house had been blown away and, right opposite, a straw-barn blazed furiously, cremating a dozen or so refugees who had been bombed while sheltering there.

It was impossible to expect the Battery, after their long hours of hard firing, to enter this charnel-house and start clearing away dead bodies to make room for the guns. Not being able to get into touch with the Major or Colonel, I decided to knock up the Divisional Commander, who dwelt in a tiny villa in the centre of Vimy, to ask him if we couldn't spend the remainder of the night in our Wagon Lines, just in front of Lens.

On the way, after crossing the Lens-Arras road, whom should I come across but the four hundred German prisoners I had seen brought into Achicourt the previous afternoon. They had been marched all the way back and were now lying asleep, dead beat, in a ditch, guarded by a few Tommies with fixed bayonets. Little groups of refugees were prowling round with decidedly hostile intentions, trying to get at the prisoners. If they happen to have escaped from the shambles at our gun-pits they may be excused their murderous passions. But the Tommies guarded their prisoners like diamonds. It was a whiff of sane old England to hear one calling out :

" Pass along, please, pass along," just as coolly as a London policeman breaking up a crowd after a street disturbance.

The Divisional Commander received me sitting on the edge of his bed, half undressed.

" Who are you ?   What do you want ? " he asked.

I informed him, and described how our Battery had been pulled out of action with German tanks only a few hundred yards away, after the enemy had overrun our infantry.

" Yes, I know about it already," he replied., " Thank heaven you got away safely."

I mentioned the gun-pits. " I don't think it is possible to ask the troops to go into those pits," I said.

He thought for a moment or two.

" Right-ho," he nodded. " Go to the Wagon Lines. Leave the map reference here so that we can inform the rest of the regiment where you are if they inquire."

Intensely relieved that I shouldn't have to look upon that piece of moonlit butchery again, I returned to the Battery rendezvous and led them to the Wagon Lines under avenues of trees on a miners' housing estate. A sergeant-major had the unpleasant job of waiting at the gun-pits till the Major turned up to explain where we had gone.

At the Wagon Lines most of the men were too weary and exhausted to dismount. They fell fast asleep in the trucks. Those that did go into the empty houses simply dropped straight down on the floor, dead to the world. I passed out in my truck, hoping to get in at least a couple of good hours before dawn broke.

It seemed that I hadn't closed my eyes when some-one, vigorously shaking my arm, awakened me. It was the sergeant-major I had left behind at the gun-pits. He brought a message from the Major. We were to go into action immediately at Givenchy. I glanced at my watch. I had been asleep one whole hour. Amazing !

Soon the sergeants were busy whipping up the slumbering troops, hauling them out of the houses, rudely bringing them back to life in the trucks. A difficult and unenviable task. Much good bad language countered the flood of remonstrance from the dog-tired men. They groused expressively in the approved manner of the British soldier ; the manner that can be safely regarded as a healthy sign.

137

" What sort of a bloody war d'you call this ? " shouted a grimy gunner with bloodshot eyes at the torturer who had so ruthlessly dragged him out of Paradise. And, overhearing it, I had no fears that we should lose much time getting on the move.

VII—On Vimy Ridge

The Major had established a Battery Command Post
at a small farmhouse in Givenchy, and thither I drove,
accompanied by the Command Post Officer and the
Gun Position Officers, to receive orders.

" You go up on the ridge near the War Memorial,"
he said to me, " and establish an O.P. to cover that
zone."

He indicated a wide front on the map from Neuville
St-Vaast on the left to Mont St-Eloi on the right.

Swallowing a few mouthfuls of fried bully beef, I
packed a tin of sardines, some bread, and a bottle of
vin rouge for future use, and departed for the ridge.
The base of the Memorial afforded a good view of the
countryside, but I decided I could do better at the
Warden's residence, a house with a tower, two hundred
yards away, stuck there on the ridge just like a little
bit of England, very un-French looking, with flower
and vegetable gardens, and a sandpit for a child.
Inside it was delightfully furnished, English style.
Perhaps I should say, had been. It made me angry
to discover how ruthlessly the interior had been
ransacked. In one room where, in happier days,
souvenir postcards had been sold, the drawers were
pulled out and looted, and the floor was a litter of
postcards and little maple leaves stamped in thin
brass. Pictures and wardrobe doors were smashed,
and sheets torn to pieces. Whether the havoc had
been caused by refugees or French troops in the
neighbourhood I could not say. I rather suspected
the latter. An hour or two later, when I was in the

tower drawing my panorama I heard the garden gate
click and saw four or five men from a French
mitrailleuse company stationed on the ridge, slinking
through the gate.

" Qui va là ? " I shouted.   " Allez-vous-en."

The alacrity with which they made off went to
confirm my suspicions.

I congratulated myself on my O.P.   The room at
the top of the Warden's tower provided a magnificent
view of the front line from the windows all round.
The ledge for the lamp used to floodlight the Memorial
supplied me with a ready-made table.   The place was
weatherproof, and a trap-door led down into an attic
where my telephonist and O.P. Ack could retire for
an occasional rest.

The pall still hung thick over the direction of Arras
to the south where the battle was raging some six
thousand yards away.   Farmhouses were burning here
and there, and occasionally red gun-flashes darted
beneath the smoke.   Otherwise there wasn't much
visible to indicate the terrific nature of the struggle
going on.   You look at a battlefield of to-day and see
no sign of the presence of the engines and agents of
modern warfare.   Yet everything is there that should
be, men and machines.   All invisible to the untutored
observer.   Suddenly a sector of the front will burst
into life.   Flashes of flame, dust and smoke rising, and
here and there a few pigmies, that are men, darting
about.   Then just as suddenly the activity peters out,
and there is nothing more to be seen.

Of course, if you are an artillery observer and you
look long enough, you do see things, some very
interesting.   A distant glint may be the sun reflected
from an enemy observer's binoculars.   And the little
rabbit's ears sticking up over the edge of a flat ridge
are quite possibly the double prongs of a German
periscope.   You suddenly see four trees where for

hours there have only been three. The new one is a
machine-gun post. A haystack begins walking. It
is a tank.

Our battlefield must have differed considerably in
appearance from the same scene of the last war. No
elaborate trench systems scarred it ; no No Man's
Land ; no extensive areas pitted with shell holes and
turned into deserts ; no acres of trees stripped, blighted
and riven. The fields appeared green and unscarred,
the woods retained their rich foliage. Only where
towns and villages dotted the landscape did the ravages
of war become explicit to the eye. Different wars,
different battlefields. And ours was moving war.
Moving at top-speed.

My day passed pretty peacefully. Quietly, too,
except for the huge flights of German bombers continually passing overhead on their way to bomb Lens.
Our guns at Givenchy were now roaring, shelling Mont
St. Eloi, and Maroeuil, which only a few hours
previously had been our own regimental headquarters.
Towards evening a special target cropped up. I
spotted a German battery of four guns in front of a
wood on the skyline. Four little equidistant flashes
gave them away. I telephoned the data to the
Battery Command Post, the targets were plotted on
the map, and as they were out of range from our
present gun positions, Ritchie, L–Troop's G.P.O., was
sent up with a section of two guns to a forward position
three miles away to conduct the strafe. His orders
were to go into action at once, fire twenty rounds per
gun at the target, and hop back again. I watched
Ritchie's tractors wind over the ridge on this errand,
just as it was getting dusk. A sergeant came along a
little later to relieve me.

" Keep a sharp look-out for the S.O.S.," I said.
" Good night ! "

Veal cutlets, tinned peas, cheddar cheese and vin

rouge awaited me at the Command Post. In the
circumstances, a Ritzian repast. But sleep was what
I needed more. It seemed years since I had had any.
I stretched myself on the floor and went off into a
profound slumber. But it wasn't deep enough to
drown the Major's voice. An hour or so later a huge
commotion awakened me. Ritchie was in the Command Post, and the Major was barking furiously down
the 'phone at someone.

"Why weren't they informed, damn it ? " I heard
him shout. "I don't send out my men to be
massacred ! "

Ritchie's little shoot had nearly ended in tragedy.
He had gone into action, fired a couple of rounds,
when without warning a battery of French 75's began
shelling him, thinking it was the enemy. Ritchie was
lucky to be able to hook in the guns, and get away
without casualties.

As I have said, the Major really let himself go over
the telephone. He had every justification, seeing that
both Regimental and Divisional Headquarters had
been warned before Ritchie set out, so as not to
mistake his guns for the enemy. But somebody had
failed to warn the French.

I murmured : "Well done, sir," when the Major
finally ran out of H.E. His had been a magnificent
effort. It fully repaid me for my broken sleep. I
closed my eyes again, and a second later knew no
more.

*   *   *   *   *

Next morning the Major astounded me. I was
having breakfast when he put his head into the room,
and said :

"You might go up to the O.P. Boyd's just telephoned down to say he's in a mix-up with the zones.
Put him right."

" Boyd ! " I exclaimed, amazed. " Boyd ! . . .
Did he get back ? "

" Trust Boyd," replied the Major, with a laugh.
" Didn't you know ? "

This was wonderful news. The last I had seen of
Boyd was at the cross-roads beyond Achicourt, the
night the German tanks broke through. We all had
given him up for lost.

Greatly cheered, I hurried to the O.P. in the
Warden's tower.

" Boyd," I said, as I put my head through the trap-
door, " I am damn glad to see you."

" Thought you would be, after the trouble you took
getting me out of Beaurains," he chuckled. " What's
this mess here ? "

He'd identified a wood wrongly on my panorama,
and it had thrown out the other points. It was easily
rectified and I stayed with him during the morning
doing some shoots. In the intervals he related his
adventures.

After I left him that night at the cross-roads, Boyd
selected a house on the road towards Achicourt for his
new O.P., parked his vehicle outside, and mounted to
the first storey. He stood on a chair to look out of
the window, and without the slightest warning found
himself in the middle of a battle. Scores of German
tanks bore down in his direction. Tracer bullets cut
up the darkness with a criss-cross of fiery streaks, and
slapped, slapped, against the walls of the house.
From just behind him came the rattle of British rifle
and machine-gun fire.

Boyd dashed down the stairs to his truck He knew
now that the way back to the battery through
Achicourt was cut off, and that his only escape
lay down the road that proceeded roughly in the
direction of Arras. He tore along for miles in
the darkness, over rough paths, gardens, fields,

through a railway siding till he emerged on a narrow
road.

" Halt ! "

He pulled up in front of a barrier, behind which a
detachment of Guards were waiting to receive the
German tanks.   He spent a quarter of an hour trying
to induce them to open the barrier.   They were willing
enough to let him through on foot, but feared that the
tanks might heave in sight at the moment they had
made a breach in the barrier wide enough for his
truck.   Finally he won, and soon afterwards found
himself in Arras, which· was deserted, heaped with
ruins, and ablaze with street fires.

Now even on a pleasant, peaceful afternoon Arras
is a funny town to drive through.   You can go round
and round in circles for hours without discovering a
way out.   Boyd, in the dead of night, amid piles of
wreckage in the roads, and streets battered out of all
recognition, made two complete circuits before, in
sheer desperation, he made a dive down a side-street
that looked fairly clear, and came out on the Arras-
Bethune road.   In front of him in the darkness proceeded a string of vehicles which he overtook, and
found to his surprise he had joined up with the tail
of Y–Battery column on its way back to Vimy.   I
had been too busy in the interval between then and
now to hear anything about it.

*   *   *   *   *

The battle line, which the afternoon before had
been roughly about 6,000 yards from the Ridge, had
by now approached to within 2,000 yards, except in
the centre where the salient towards Arras still jutted
out.   From each flank the roar and rattle of the fighting grew in intensity.   You could see the tracer shells
of the anti-tank guns firing at the German tanks quite
plainly, and the spurts of machine-gun fire, and tiny

figures of men running hither and thither every now and then, in and out of the curtain of smoke.

We did a couple of useful shoots that morning. An enemy tank concentration was reported in a wood near Mont St. Eloi. We worked the target out off the map and fired a salvo which apparently caught the tanks just as they were emerging from the wood. Four out of the twelve were knocked out, and the others retreated. Later on we shelled big enemy infantry concentrations in Mont St. Eloi itself, watching through our glasses with great satisfaction our own shells bursting in their midst.

Another pleasant surprise met me when I returned to the Command Post.

" Your truck's been rescued," said the A.C.P.O. " The Green Howards brought it in. It's over in our workshops now. They must have known how sick you were to lose your mascot. I'm told they fought a desperate engagement with enemy tanks to salvage it for you," he went on, chaffing.

The official diagnosis of the truck trouble that had so nearly landed me into the hands of the Germans was : " Transmission half shot away in machine-gun attack by the Messerschmitts ; extra strain when violently turning at sight of German tank just ahead had caused it to snap. Signed, M.T.O. (Mechanical Transport Officer.)"

My truck came back to the battery in due course, windscreen in perfect perforated condition. I counted the bullet holes. They were all there. Not one missing. The entire thirteen !

VIII—GIVENCHY GROWS UNHEALTHY

Judged simply on its own merits, there was nothing
to be said against the Command Post at Givenchy.
It was in a very comfortable farmhouse with a pretty
courtyard and, what was more desirable, an excellent
cellar (not for wine !). The same, however, could not
be said about Givenchy itself. Hour by hour the
atmosphere became more ominous. It was now that
we first grew conscious that we were all the time
under observation by unseen eyes. We felt like the
mouse in the shadow of a cat, every moment expecting
a pounce. This uncomfortable feeling was never
really to leave us again. German reconnaissance planes
dogged us everywhere,' photographing our positions
without any opposition in the air. We even got to
the stage of believing one special plane had been given
charge of us. The routine was always the same :
Reconnaissance plane circling overhead. Reconnaissance
plane flies off. Dive bombers two hours later. The
marvel was that we did not have very heavy casualties.

So when the Major, at lunch, remarked that the air
of the place struck him as getting decidedly unhealthy
we agreed unanimously. During that same morning
the bombers had knocked out a Bofors anti-aircraft
position in the centre of our gun positions, scoring two
direct hits on the emplacement. A little later a
detachment of French tanks took it into their heads
to halt in the middle of the village. They were
spotted, and another wave of bombers zoomed up
They missed the tanks but hit a cartload of refugees,
thus blocking up the main street.

You can guess the sweet thoughts of the Major, therefore, when half-way through lunch another gunner regiment, coming out of action into positions farther back, halted the whole of one battery right in the middle of Givenchy. Part of the vehicles parked outside the front door of our Command Post.

The Major dashed out and caught the first subaltern he could find.

" Look," he shouted angrily, " you are bloody fools ! You're asking to be bombed. Can't you move somewhere else ? After all, we've got to live here."

They took no notice. And just as we were about to have coffee, the whine of the first dive-bomber was heard. For five minutes Givenchy rocked. When it was over a strange thing happened. The usual un-earthly silence that succeeds a dive-bombing attack did not materialise. Instead, there commenced a series of odd, irregular explosions. Besides getting a direct hit on the church, the bombers had dropped a couple of bombs plump on two of the ammunition trailers parked outside our front door, setting them on fire. Shells and charges were exploding, bits flying in all directions.

The offending battery had pushed off while the raid was still on, leaving behind the wrecked trailers. So the Major was deprived of the satisfaction of telling them what he really did think of them. For the remainder of the afternoon Givenchy was a dangerous place to walk about in. You stood a good chance of being killed by a British shell.

*   *   *   *   *

More unrest in the afternoon. Regimental Head-quarters in a farm a mile behind Givenchy was machine-gunned by low-flying aircraft and a gunner killed. Even more disturbing was the news that they were being sniped from the right. A patrol went out, but failed to find anything. In the Battery we put it down to stray Fifth Column work.

We took another view when the Major returned from R.H.Q. conference early in the evening.

" I'm thirsty. Cup of tea going ? " he said quietly, and in the same tone continued : " The French on our right have fallen back, and left us exposed. We've got to make a side-step, giving up the part of the ridge we're now holding. We're to go to the other side of the Lens-Arras road and come into action at Thelus."

I was ordered to reconnoitre a " hide " for the Battery in the area of Fresnoy-en-Gohelle.

" Come back by the same route," said the Major, " and if the battery is out of action it will be coming along that way, and you can take it back to the hide."

I found a " hide " in the grounds of a château outside the village. It was even more " ideal " than the Wagon-Lines Officer's at Anzin St. Aubin—and without shell-holes. A French mechanised Cavalry Regiment were already in possession, but there was room for us.

I retraced my course, passed through Vimy, and had nearly reached the Battery position when I ran into British infantry forming a line at right angles to the line we had just been holding. This was a bit of a revelation. It meant the enemy were pushing forward rapidly on our right flank.

" What's doing in front ? " I asked.

No one seemed to know. Information was very scanty. But it was understood that the head of a German motorised column was in Givenchy, barely a mile away.

I began to feel anxious about the Battery. Had they got out in time ? And at that moment they came round a bend in the road. I waved them forward, turned my truck, and led them along to the " hide."

A French mechanised column had now joined the

road. As usual, no march discipline, very disorderly, and living up to the French Army's motto on the move : " Get there anyhow, as soon as possible, and don't bother about pushing other people off the road."

So we had to force our way through inconceivable confusion. And when I arrived at the " hide " half the Battery was missing. They had been unable to disentangle themselves from the maelstrom.

While the Major went off with the reconnaissance officers to examine our new positions, I returned along the route in search of the missing guns. In the pitch-black night I could discover no trace of them. Farm-houses and barns were burning in the distance ; and not so distant either. Coming back through Méricourt I found it crowded with French infantry on the retreat, very tired and dirty, very disorderly, display-ing days of beard, bits of wet cigarettes hanging from their lips. I remember thinking how philosophical they appeared to take things ; and then, that it wasn't philosophy at all, but a rather ominous sort of in-difference.

Outside Méricourt I turned a bend in the road. Coming direct at me, and doing at least fifty miles an hour was a motor-cyclist. There was no chance for my driver to avoid him. He hit us head-on with a terrific crash that lifted the truck off its front wheels and flung me against the wind-screen. When I could use my eyes again, both rider and machine had dis-appeared.

The motor-cycle was right under the truck, and the man half-under. Pulling him out, I saw he was a Don R. I flashed my torch and found to my consterna-tion that he was one of our own men—a sergeant from R.H.Q. attached to Division.

The poor fellow was in agony and half-unconscious.

" Is that you, Captain ——", he gasped, recognising

me in the torch light. " It's my legs, sir. They're both smashed."

Then, coming out of another faint, he murmured :

" Important message in my right-hand pocket."

I felt, drew out a pink message telegram, opened it and held it close to the torch.

" TEMO I to NOFE I," I read. That meant from the Divisional Commander to our Colonel. The message read :

> " WITHDRAW TO HOUPLIN. ROUTE, HENIN-LIETARD, CARVIN, SECLIN."

Urgent ! I should just think it was. A complete reversal of the orders received earlier in the evening to come into action.

Not only that. I knew that Houplin was about thirty miles away, up in the north near Lille.

A startling piece of intelligence to leap out of the black night at one in such grim circumstances.

I made the sergeant as comfortable as I could by the roadside, and sent my driver into Mericourt to bring back a French doctor.

" You'll be all right," I whispered to the injured man. " I've sent for help."

Giving him a hand-shake, I started to run back to the " hide " with the message, my truck being smashed. However, an infantry Colonel came along and gave me a lift. I despatched a Don R. from the " hide " to R.H.Q. with the message, and to ask the Colonel what I should do about it, as the Major and several officers were out on reconnaissance.

IX—One Night of the Retreat

" You see if I'm not right. We'll be on our way back to England within a fortnight," said the A.C.P.O.

I shall always regard that as an amazing bit of prophecy. The A.C.P.O. brewed it as we stood at the cross-roads outside the " hide " discussing with Boyd the dramatic turn in the situation. British troops were now arriving at the cross-roads in ever-increasing numbers. They converged from south, east, and west, all with faces turned to the north. One road remained open—the road to Henin-Liétard. And they poured down it as down a funnel. From passing infantry officers we picked up what news we could. But it was mostly rumour, or vague statements such as : " The Germans are three parts round us." One report that the enemy had taken the Ridge, which overlooked our country, struck me as very likely true.

Nevertheless, there was nothing in all this to encourage anyone to embark on prophecy as far-flung as the A.C.P.O.'s. True we were retreating, and retreating fast. We were also retreating north. We were even retreating towards the Channel ports, perhaps. But still, that was a very different thing from being " on our way back to England within a fortnight."

We howled with laughter at the A.C.P.O.

Suddenly the C.R.A. (Commandant, Royal Artillery) of the Nth Division, a Brigadier with two scarlet silk buttons on the collar of his battledress, approached us out of the darkness. He knew me.

" What are you doing here ? " he asked.

I informed him my Battery was in a hide up the road.

" Take my advice and get them on that road quick," he said. " In another half an hour it will be choked. Use clear road, my lad, while you've got the chance."

I explained that the Major was out on a reconnaissance, and that I was waiting orders from the Colonel.

" Well, I should move on," he urged.

" If I do will you take the responsibility ? "

" Yes, yes. I'll take the responsibility. You get off now."

Boyd and the A.C.P.O. volunteered to remain behind to tell the Major we'd gone. The word was passed to the drivers to start up, and with just a pin-point of a tail-light showing, we turned into the Henin-Liétard road.

It was midnight, very dark, the moon not yet having risen. After a while we got in behind the Staff vehicles of the Nth Division, and trailed them till, at a road junction, an R.A.S.C. Supply Column got in between us. Then followed a big hold-up at a cross-roads where a French Army Corps in trucks and lorries took possession, flinging everything into confusion, careering along in the blackness three abreast, shoving everyone else off the road into the ditch.

Mile after mile down the road the column grew and grew, and crawled and crawled. Everyone was worn-out for want of sleep. Drivers kept going mechani-cally, the movement just sufficient to keep them awake and no more. If an enforced halt occurred, however brief, they dropped sound asleep in their seats instantly. When we moved on a bit, many of the drivers remained asleep. The column proceeded, leaving them behind, blocking the road. Traffic Con-trol of the Divisional Staff, and the C.M.P. (Military Police) then chased up and down the road in the darkness waking up the delinquents in no gentle fashion.

" Wake up, blast you. . . ."

" Get moving, you bastard. . . ."

" You're holding the whole bloody column up, curse you. . . ."

Officers and men, they ll got it alike. A blinding torch flashed in the sleep s face, then—salvo.

On through what had been Henin-Liétard. The bombers had left little of it standing. Piles of broken masonry and rubble choked the roads. The main avenue was impassable, so the column wriggled through side-streets so narrow that the guns were forced on to the pavements. A sort of dry rasping noise kept us company ; the hard crunch of wheels on the carpet of broken glass.

On to Carvin. And here another petrifying horror. One of those appalling spectacles that, like the shambles in our Vimy gun-pits, strike the heart cold. Something transcending even the normal imagined horrors of War.

Behind some railings in the main street stood a red-brick convent school that had been badly bombed. And spread out on the wide white pavement in front were the bodies of sixty victims, all girls between the ages of fifteen and seventeen. The corpses had been arranged in four regular rows, one behind the other on the broad flags. There they lay, rigid and motionless in the moonlight, staring up at the sky, exactly like a Company that had formed fours and then fallen down flat on their backs. The mathematical precision of the arrangement added to the terror of the scene. You could fancy yourself looking upon the devilish finale of some marionette show—" Death's Drill," or " Death by Numbers." To heighten the horrible, unhuman aspect of this pavement mortuary, the faces, bare arms, and legs were discoloured by a ghastly mauve tint, the result, probably, of shock or blast from the bomb. Perhaps the bodies had been laid-out in this pattern for identification and collection by relatives. But there was little chance of this. All the living inhabitants of the village had fled. Not a soul dared remain to watch over and guard the mauve-faced dead. Alone, deserted, there they lay on their backs. Alone, with their wide-eyed appeal to the Heavens.

Thousands and thousands of the troops were lucky enough to pass through Carvin that night without seeing them. By now we were approximating an army asleep on wheels. Hardly anybody but was dozing all the time, as nose to tail, the column jerked, crawled and rumbled on its way. Drivers only woke up with a start when going round corners, or when they hit a kerb. Then relapsed into a doze again. The road was now one solid mass of vehicles, British and French, almost indistinguishable from each other in the darkness ; tanks, artillery columns, Bren-gun carriers and infantry trucks.

Progress had been so tortoise-like throughout the night, that instead of Y-Battery getting to its " hide " at Houplin in the dark, as hoped, we were still many miles off when dawn began to steal very quickly over the flat horizon. Now began an anxious time. It would soon be daylight. We should become visible from the air. The ideal target for the German bombers. Two British Divisions and most of the transport of a French Army Corps, all jumbled up on a fairly narrow road, the mix-up stretching for miles and miles, no gaps, all the vehicles nose to tail, and crawling along at the pace of an active snail. It was impossible to keep one's eyes from the skies as the daylight strengthened. I don't know what the Divisional Commanders thought. Probably the same as us—that we were for it.

For this reason the rest of the drive through Seclin, which the bombs had knocked to bits, was a daylight nightmare. Sure enough, a German reconnaissance

154

plane appeared overhead. And it looked as if nothing could save us.

At last, with a huge sigh of relief we reached the side-road where Y-Battery was to leave the threatened column and turn left to Houplin. I stood at the corner of the road, signalling each vehicle to turn as it came up. They were so strung out and mixed up with the rest of the column that this promised to be a long job. The C.R.A. of the Mth Division, a charming man. walked up and stood beside me. He had halted to watch his division go by.

" Amazing sight, isn't it ? " he said. It was indeed, even to the weariest of eyes ; pale daylight revealing this great war caravan stretching mile after mile over the road as far as the eye could see.

" Look at that."

In front of us was passing another gunner regiment. One of its guns had had all its balloon tyres shot away, and was being dragged along by the trailer on its brake drums.

" Your service number is 5, isn't it ? " said the C.R.A.

All our vehicles had a white 5 painted on a red and blue background. It was our regimental number.

" If you'd like to go on," said the C.R.A. " I'll turn your vehicles off the road as they come along. I shall be here for some time."

Coming from a C.R.A. this was pretty good. I accepted gladly.

Houplin, for a change, hadn't been bombed. It was the first village I had seen for days unscarred by War. The sight was as refreshing to the eyes as is a drink of water to a parched throat. Here in this pretty red agricultural village, planted amid its flat fields, a bit of Peace still lingered. Or so it seemed.

Anyhow, my first impressions were very favourable.

Oh, yes. It had taken us over ten hours to do the thirty-mile journey.

X—BLEMISHES ON A BEAUTY-SPOT

The Colonel met me at the entrance to the village.

" Most of the Battery is behind me, sir," I reported.
" The rest are coming along."

" Right. Take them to the ' hide.' Go straight
along this road. You'll come to a wood on the left.
You'll see a white gate. Go in there."

The white gates led into an avenue through the
grounds of a charming and picturesque house—half-
château, half-farm—covered with wistaria, whose old
weathered tile-roof was daubed in coloured lichens
and mosses like a painter's palette. Against the background of brilliant blue sky and cotton-wool clouds, it
appeared a most delectable spot. An oasis in the
desert of War. Half a dozen sleek well-fed horses
frisked in a paddock near the clump of trees that was
to be our " hide." Parked on either side of the main
avenue were two or three ambulances containing
wounded, and some R.A.S.C. vehicles which had
arrived earlier in the morning.

As we drove inside the delight of the picture was
considerably enhanced by the appearance of a very
pretty blue-eyed blonde girl, not more than twenty.
She emerged from a cowshed carrying a milk pail, a
red handkerchief tied round her head in gipsy fashion,
and waved to us with a smile. She was one of the
twin daughters of the old farmer, who with his wife
and family was carrying-on as if such a thing as War
never existed.

She put the finishing touch to Houplin. We decided
we liked the place very much.

An hour or two passed. At last the Major turned up. He was still fuming with indignation over his experience on the road. When he returned to the " hide " at Fresnoy-en-Gohelle the previous night, Boyd and the A.C.P.O. delivered my message and the Major started off at full speed in his truck up the Henin-Liétard road to overtake the Battery, passing the slowly winding column on the outer side wherever he could. Unfortunately for him, the Nth Division had a rooted objection to double-banking. You simply *had* to keep in the column. So the Major, tearing along in the darkness, suddenly found himself at a traffic control point with somebody waving a torch in his face.

" Put that bloody torch out ! " he yelled.

" Stop, or I shoot ! " came the stern reply.

The Major thrust his head out of the truck and found himself confronted by the C.R.A., of all people. And the C.R.A. held his revolver in his hand.

" There's no use panicking," said the C.R.A. harshly.

This was more than the Major could stand from anyone. He uncorked like a bottle of champagne.

" Panicking be damned ! " he shouted. " I'm trying to catch up my Battery."

" Never mind that," said the C.R.A. firmly. " You've got to pull in."

And the Major had to squeeze himself into the first little gap that occurred and crawl along with the rest of the queue.

I commiserated with him, and he strolled off towards the main entrance with the C.P.O. Hardly was his back turned when the drone of a 'plane sounded overhead. Before one had time to think a bomb burst with a terrific explosion fifty yards away.

The Major came running back.

" Quick ! " he shouted. " All fire extinguishers, axes and hatchets. And all the men."

The bomb had fallen in the avenue. Some supply lorries were wrecked and two ambulances were blazing. The wounded were pulled out on their stretchers and placed a safe distance off. The ground was strewn with the bodies of a dozen R.A.S.C. and R.A.M.C. men, dead and dying. One of Y–Battery's drivers, who had been late in leaving the column, was killed instantaneously while driving his ammunition trailer through the gates. He was buried in the grounds, and our fitters made a very handsome wooden cross to mark the spot.

The entire Battery helped to extinguish the flames and salvage the supplies. I'm afraid we regarded the latter in the light of a heaven-sent opportunity. Tins of peas, potatoes, biscuits, sugar, tea went to replenish our own depleted larder. Our mechanics had the time of their lives salvaging odd tools and spare electric light bulbs. They were able to completely re-fit their workshops with new spare parts.

That bomb wrought a sudden psychological change in Y–Battery. Our beautiful " hide " assumed a sinister atmosphere. We felt very conscious of Death lurking round the corner. Like being in a trap baited with beauty. Were we in a trap ?

No one felt very happy. But we were too worn out to worry much. Sleep was all we craved for. Sleep, and more sleep. We flung ourselves down where we stood and passed out. The G.P.O. of M–Battery put up a record for the whole regiment. He fell down on the straw in a barn face downwards, and never moved for sixteen hours.

*   *   *   *   *

Next morning I awoke with a dim idea that something had happened to me. I couldn't fix it for hours. Then I remembered it was my birthday. That meant a bath in the " private " hip-bath I had convoyed

with so much care all the way from Wortegem. I had
promised myself this as a birthday treat. And, as
luck would have it, here we were with a breathing
space. For days and days I had been dreaming
lovingly of that bath, roped to the ammunition trailer.
Had I not dragged it for over two hundred miles
without having a chance of using it ?

My servant approached. " Bad news, sir," he said
solemnly. " That bomb yesterday got our bath."

" Are you sure ? " I exclaimed, horrified.

" Certain, sir. Mr. Ritchie told me to inform you."

" He would," I said bitterly, remembering Wortegem.

So my cherished birthday present to myself was
gone. I discovered that a bomb splinter had knocked
the bottom out of it. Nothing else on the trailer had
been touched except, of course, the unfortunate driver.

There still remained another celebration.

" It's my birthday," I said to the Wagon Lines
Officer.

" Forgotten there are such things," he replied.
" Champagne ? "

" Yes. See if you can get some for me."

He procured six bottles of Pommard, also a cake,
from an old man he discovered lurking in a cellar in
devastated Seclin. It was loot, I expect. But the
Wagon Lines Officer, flush with my money, paid West
End night-club prices for it. The six stalwarts made
a brave show on the table when the Mess came in to
lunch.

" Who's that on ? " everybody asked quickly.

" Me. It's my birthday. For dinner to-night."

" Not on your life," said Tops, N–Troop Commander.
" We daren't take the risk. Don't you know there's a
war on ? Any moment a wine-waiter may drop from
the skies bang into the middle of that champagne.
And he won't be bringing ice. No, I prefer to do
my own uncorking. Besides, we may have to move

off suddenly, and there won't be any dinner. I know it's your birthday, old fellow, but I can't allow you to ruin it out of innocence."

It was decided we should have three bottles at once, and the remainder at dinner.

The day wore on, very hot and oppressive. Nerves were a bit on edge. We grew more and more vaguely suspicious of our beauty spot. To begin with, a sergeant reported that the previous night he had seen lights flashing from a top room in the farmhouse. The Hooker, Ritchie and myself planned a spy hunt for to-night.

Later in the afternoon came a parachutist scare. Several of the troops swore to having seen something drop out of a 'plane not far away. The Hooker, the C.P.O. and Boyd went off with an armed party to beat a wood. They searched high and low, found nothing, and the C.P.O., becoming very bored, took a pot-shot with his revolver at a water-rat. Immediately they were down on their faces. The wood sprang to life with the rattle of musketry. Bullets whizzed over their heads from each side. And they returned the fire.

As it happened, a French patrol was also in the wood, searching for the parachutist. A party of British infantry was out on the same errand. Hearing the C.P.O.'s shot, each thought the enemy was at hand. Everybody began firing on each other. After two or three minutes the firing died down. We were rather relieved at the " hide " when our party returned to discover that it was not forward German troops who had found us at last, but merely a private war started by the C.P.O.

It all shows how touchy we were getting.

Then there were the Major's continual visits to the Colonel. Obviously something was doing. The complete absence of definite information about the enemy

that was worrying the Colonel and the Major began
to disturb us. One of its periodical morbid moods
descended on the Mess at dinner. Even the champagne couldn't drown it. We sat listening to sporadic
rifle and machine-gun fire. In the still of the night
it didn't sound very far away. Then a battery of
French heavy guns came into action, not half a mile off.

"That sounds pretty close," said the Major, and
again went off to see the Colonel.

This time he brought back news.

"We've got to stay here the night," he said.
"They've sent out a patrol of two officers who found
the Germans are in Seclin, working round to our left.
But Division hasn't yet given us orders to move.
Although they definitely know the situation now. Be
prepared to move first thing in the morning."

*   *   *   *   *

After this it was quite a relief to begin our spy
hunt. At half-past ten, when it was quite dark, the
Hooker, Ritchie and myself, with a couple of armed
sergeants, crept quietly round the farmhouse. Sure
enough there was a light shining from a top window
at the back of the house. Over that flat country-
side it must have been visible for miles. The Hooker
and I hammered on the front door. After a while
the old farmer appeared in his nightshirt. Curtly, we
demanded an explanation of that light.

The old farmer was desolé. Messieurs les Capitaines
could take his word for it that it was a very unfortunate
accident. Someone had forgotten to turn the electric
light off at the main. He himself would go down to
the cellar and do it immediately.

We walked round to the back of the house and
waited. In a few seconds the light disappeared.

"Let's get back to bed now," said the Hooker.
And we were just moving off when a light flashed in

the room again. This time a moving light, as if someone was signalling.

" Cover that window with your rifles," ordered the Hooker to the two sergeants, and then thundered out : " Surrender, or we'll fire."

Instantly the window was flung up and a head thrust out.

" Don't be such a blasted fool," shouted an anxious voice. " It's me."

It was Ritchie. While we were at the front door he had sloped off to conduct a private investigation on his own. Somehow he made his way into the house and crept up to the top room. Opening the door he found himself in darkness. So he flashed on his torch and began to search under the vacant bed. He found nothing. And then came the Hooker's startling challenge.

We returned to the Mess convinced it was not spies. But before falling to sleep I grew unconvinced again. And it was around the blonde twins that my suspicions revolved. With that flaxen hair and those blue eyes they reminded one of a couple of typical Saxon Gretchens. There was this in their favour, though. They weren't plump.

*   *   *   *   *

No undressing that night. Reveille was at 5 a.m. A quick breakfast off hard-boiled eggs. The guns were hooked in. Engines were warmed up. All ready to pull out.

Half an hour later a Don R. brought a message to the Major from R.H.Q.

" Call the other officers," he said to me, and addressed us : " We are moving back to Estaires. Route via Ligny and Fromelles. Pace fifteen miles in the hour. Ten vehicles to the mile. All vehicles nose to tail till the gate is passed, and then spread out on the road."

A curious but well-defined sense of relief seized hold of me as I led the Battery away from that beautiful old farmhouse. The two blonde sisters stood outside the door, smiling and waving good-bye to us. Again I thought it stupid to harbour suspicions. Still . . .

We wound through the village, turned left, on towards the bridge over the canal, and, just as we approached, between twenty and thirty German bombers roared overhead. I felt certain they were going for the bridge. But without any more ado they dive-bombed our late " hide " to hell. Fortunately the last of our vehicles had just cleared the gate.

Not yet have I made up my mind about those blonde girls.

XI—We Learn We are Prayed For

It rained at Estaires. The fact is worth recording because it was the first and last drop of rain we saw throughout the Invasion. It almost took us by surprise. More unexpected than dive-bombers! Otherwise our days had been one long succession of blazing suns, usually striking down hard from a cloudless sky. Our faces, necks and arms exhibited a brick-red tan, which if it weren't exactly the fashionable Riviera hue, did wonderful credit to the ultra-violet rays we had absorbed. And the water-cart could never put in an appearance too soon.

We were now in a district where at every turn some reminiscence of our fathers' war mingled with the brand-new havoc of our own. Estaires, Laventie, Neuve Chapelle, Festubert—hardly one of these villages possessed a house built before 1919. Some of them had been constructed so as to incorporate one of the concrete pill-boxes of " slow-motion " war days to be used as a store-house. Dotted over the flat marshy fields, where the cows stood knee-deep in lush grass, were isolated pill-boxes that had half-subsided into the soft ground. Iron " corkscrews," that held the barbed wire in the last war, now formed part of the fencing to keep the cows from straying. For miles and miles there was hardly a tree to be seen more than twelve feet high. The entire country had to be replanted after the guns of 1914–1918 finished with it. And here were the dive-bombers of 1940 already cutting short these youngsters' brief spell of existence.

It was at Estaires, too, that we grew conscious of a decided hardening of the German pressure on us. The invisible ring seemed to be closer, and tighter. We felt, if we did not know, that they were right on our heels, though we had withdrawn thirty miles north. Their planes, of course, had never left us alone. But now we could smell their tanks and armoured cars again.

Just outside the village we turned down a road to our billeting area, splitting the Battery up among four fair-sized farms, and some cottages, and hiding the guns in barns. Strict instructions were issued to the troops not to walk about in the open more than was necessary. The German eyes in the air were too sharp to encourage us to take even slight chances.

During the afternoon the Major returned from a conference with the Colonel in Estaires. His news confirmed our foreboding.

" The situation is serious," he said. " Reports have come in that advanced German armoured fighting vehicles are in the neighbourhood. We must immediately make tank blocks on this part of the road. We'll be stopping here the night. Or part, at least. When we do move we shall probably come into action somewhere in the Ypres area. I don't know where yet."

Old farm-carts, rusty ploughshares, farm implements, broken doors, lumps of brick and concrete, were gathered from all quarters and piled higgledy-piggledy across the road, where they formed a respectable barrier. Anti-tank rifles and Bren guns were placed on either side, covering the obstacle with their fire. But afternoon and evening passed without further alarm.

I shared with the Major a room in the farm-house containing two single beds. That night we went to sleep dressed except for our blouses, as we expected to be off at any moment.

It was half-past three in the morning when the Major's servant shook him out of a lovely deep slumber.

" You're wanted at R.H.Q. immediately, sir," he said.

" Blast it ! " cursed the Major, irritably, putting on his boots by the light of a torch.

Snatching up his map and notebook he hurried out of the door, calling to me as he disappeared :

" Wake the others up in case we have to move quickly."

I cursed in my turn. So did all the others except the A.C.P.O., who sleepily sat up in bed with a blanket wrapped round him, looking rather like a decayed chrysalis.

" Is there any real need to get up ? " he expostulated, in familiar Sunday-morning-at-home style.

The Major was back very quickly.

" Be ready to move in an hour," he said.

The Troops were ordered to hook-in. We snatched a quick breakfast of tea and biscuits, while the Major went into details.

" We're going into action west of Ypres," he said. " Probably near Vlamertinghe. Route will be Erquinghem-Nieppe-Neuve Eglise, along the Poperinghe road, and turn off towards Vlamertinghe."

He gave us a map reference of our probable " hide." But there had been no time to decide on anything definite. No " hide " had yet been reconnoitred. The Wagon Lines Officer was to go on ahead accompanied by a sergeant on a motor-cycle to see to this. We should receive details while on the march.

" Our Division is to hold the ground in front of Ypres on a line running along the Ypres-Comines canal," continued the Major. " The Belgian army, which is on a front at right-angles to our new line, is going to move across our front from right to left. When it gets to our left flank it is going to pivot. That will bring it right round to form a continuous line with us to the sea.

" So if you see armoured cars or troops moving across the front, be damn careful they're Germans, not Belgians, before opening fire. We have to be in action by 3 p.m."

I considered we'd made a happy start when the Battery was safely over the bridge at Erquinghem. We were always glad to get over bridges after having witnessed that mess at Oudenarde. The dive-bombers had been busy at Erquinghem just before we arrived, but had missed the bridge. Bomb craters pitted the banks at either end of it.

On to Nieppe, a suburb of Armentières, over which city now hung a thick dirty-grey blanket of smoke that told its own tale. We had seen the flights of bombers pass over us at Estaires on their way to bomb Armentières. Our interest in its fate was a very personal one. Not a man of Y–Battery but had formed friendships and associations during the happy four months in billets there. Yes, we sorrowed for Armentières under its funeral pall yonder. The A.C.P.O. contrived to make a swift dash into the city to get some supplies and bring back news. The bombing had been mercilessly thorough. Armentières was a smoking ruin. The street from the Hotel de Ville to the railway station lay completely flat. The great mansion with the marble halls and gold bath-taps that had been our R.H.Q. was no more. Our old Battery Office had received a direct hit. Dead and dying filled the streets, many of the bodies half-hanging out of the windows. Underground cellars filled with refugees had been bombed, and those who had not been killed outright were drowned in the floods that followed.

" What about my billet ? " I asked the A.C.P.O.

" All right," he replied. " But there isn't an inch of glass left in it."

It was consoling to know that, at least, the walls of one pleasant family home still remained standing in that city of wreckage.

At Nieppe we passed the red-and-white frontier barrier, and found ourselves in Belgium for the second time since the Invasion. Here we joined up with the traffic of a British Division—guns, ambulances, R.A.S.C. and R.A.M.C. vehicles, infantry trucks—all pouring back from the south. It was a broiling day. Not a speck in the magnificent blue sky except the batches of German planes flying over towards Ypres. Then came the thud, thud, thud of the explosions, and they sounded quite close.

Suddenly the entire column was brought to a halt. It looked like being a prolonged one. The A.C.P.O. and I went across to sit in the shade in a farmyard on the opposite side of the road. Unfortunately, the Battery had been forced to pull up near some cross-roads. Some of the vehicles were, in fact, actually on this danger spot.

In the farmyard the A.C.P.O. and I began chatting about the subject uppermost in all minds at that moment—What was going to happen ?

" Remember my prophecy at Fresnoy ? " he said.

" Yes. And it still makes me laugh," I answered.

" Well, if we're not on the road to England, where are we bound for ? "

" Probably going to hold a salient based on the Channel ports and stretching down as far as Lille."

" Any authority ? "

" My deduction from something I heard the C.R.A. drop."

The A.C.P.O. was silent for a moment.

" It's all damn puzzling," he mused. " You can't

get a line on anything from anybody. The infantry
don't know anything either. Much less than we do.
And have you noticed the significant change that has
taken place in official terminology ? "

" What ?"

" Down there at Vimy, the word was always ' side-
stepping,' never ' withdrawal.' When we had to go
back we were just ' side-stepping ' the Germans. But
now there's no longer any attempt to keep up that
pretence. It's ' withdrawal ' all right, now—Official.
Next, I suppose, it will be ' retreat.' "

But here the A.C.P.O. went wrong. " Retreat "
never became official.

Whing . . . Boom . . . ! A shell landed in a field
about thirty yards away.

" Must be a stray ack-ack shell," I said casually.

Hardly had I spoken when over came another. It
burst a few yards behind my truck. Then two more
high velocity small shells crashed on the other side of
the farmhouse.

We were well on our feet by now. " Get the vehicles
off the cross-roads," shouted the A.C.P.O. " They've
been spotted."

The A.C.P.O. dashed in one direction, I in another.
The sudden shelling had flung the column into consternation. All the drivers leaped from their vehicles
and disappeared into ditches. Just as the A.C.P.O.
approached one truck it received a direct hit. This
was really a ghastly tragedy. The truck contained
all the Battery records, and the Office stationery. It
also contained 125,000 cigarettes, the entire Battery
stock. This was the tragedy.

I thought it safer to run across the fields to get to
the vehicles at the other side of the cross-roads. A
whistling flutter sounded in the air as another shell
came in my direction. I flattened-out on the ground.
The shell burst a cricket-pitch in front of me, pelting

me with clods of soft earth. I jumped up and scurried on. Another crash, this time the length of a cricket-pitch behind me. I was seized with the nasty illusion that the Germans could actually see me, and were bracketing me.

Then I heard the A.C.P.O.'s warning shout :

" Quick. The column's moving."

I raced back across the fields to my truck, and we began to beat up the drivers, the sergeants ferreting them out of the ditches with threats and curses. If we didn't get a move on we should be holding up half the Divisional Column on a road that was being shelled. The urgency of the moment excused all the language that was employed.

" Out of that ditch, you bloody coward. . . ."

" Where's So-and-So ? Why isn't he with his truck ! Find the b——. He ought to be bloody well shot."

In the middle of the tumult another shell burst ten yards away from the A.C.P.O. I could hardly believe my eyes when I looked again and saw him still standing up, unhurt and unmoved.

The column got into motion with shells still dropping round. A couple of dozen rounds all told had been fired in those hectic few minutes. A parting shot graced our clearance of the cross-roads.

On reaching Neuve Eglise we discovered the reason for the sudden halt. Neuve Eglise had just been bombed flat. These were the explosions we heard a short while previously. So high was the wreckage piled in the streets that the ordinary routes through the village were impassable. The column was held up while the C.M.P.'s marked new by-passes with paper arrows through side-streets. Trucks were full of wounded men receiving attention from the R.A.M.C.

On through Neuve Eglise, skirting the base of Mt. Kemmel which sticks up like a great pimple in the flat plain, and down the Poperinghe road. Just before reaching the spot where we were to turn off for Vlamertinghe a sergeant came towards me. He had been stationed there to meet me by the Major.

" Alteration to route, sir," said the sergeant, giving me details of a new road we were to take round by Dickebusch.

" Why ? "

" The road is under shell fire, sir. The enemy is only a mile and a half away."

We turned off towards Dickebusch, and a little way down the road a German plane hedge-hopped right over us. Much to our surprise and contentment it flew off without paying us any attention. This particular area was very much afflicted by hedge-hopping just then, the planes concentrating upon machine-gunning the infantry.

Finally we reached our temporary " hide " by the side of a wood. Higher up the road stood the Colonel giving instructions to the Major. It was the first time I had seen him for days and I was struck by the serious look on his face. The Major beckoned me to approach.

" Will you bring the Battery on to here," he said, pointing to cross-roads on the map. " They are being shelled," he added, " so come across at intervals."

Once again I put the Battery into motion. Shells were bursting around the cross-roads as we approached. One fell on the road itself and another in a field by the side. For extra safety we strung out to a distance of two hundred yards between each vehicle, and on nearing the hot spot put on full speed.

My truck, at the head of the Battery, simply leaped along the road. Driving into shell-fire produces an entirely different sensation from being under it. I was chiefly conscious of feeling the skin on my face become almost painfully tight, as if it were being extended by pressure from within and obstinately refused to stretch any more. When I found myself

safe the other side of the cross-roads, it really hurt me
to separate my jaws, so hard had I clenched them
unconsciously at the moment of making my dash
forward.

We were lucky at that cross-roads. All the vehicles
came over without a scratch. Shells either burst a
second or two too early, or else too late. The same
could never have happened again.

After passing through Dickebusch we turned off
the road and went into our " hide," four miles from
Vlamertinghe, in an orchard, just as at Neder Brakel
when we went into action in Belgium for the first time.
The ages that seemed to separate those two orchards !
Really, it was less than two weeks.

It was now about one o'clock. The Colonel and
the Major departed on a reconnaissance of the gun
areas. The cooks busied themselves with preparations
for a much-needed lunch. We had eaten nothing since
tea and biscuits just before quitting Estaires at 5 a.m.

" I'm going to see if I can find out what's happening
in the world," said Boyd. And he walked off to tell
his wireless operator to tune-in to the news.

Within five minutes.I saw him coming back to me,
his lips pressed very firmly together as always, when
he wanted to register coolness though really inwardly
much moved.

" D'you know they've been praying for us in
England ? " he said.

" Why not ? We're a sinful lot," I replied easily,
not catching immediately his drift.

" You don't understand," he said impatiently.
" This is the big thing. Archbishops and all that.
Prayers for our safety in every church and cathedral
in the land. A National Day of Prayer, they called it."

" Prayers for *our* safety ? " I echoed incredulously.
" We're not in any danger. Or are we ? "

He did not reply, and we stared at one another.

XII—" The Belgians Have Packed Up "

No doubt about the shock to all of us. Of course, for some days we had realised we were up against a bit of hard trouble. We knew, too, that it was the sort of trouble that might sprout unexpected surprises. We'd had a bad time and we might have worse. But we had too much faith in the B.E.F. to believe that anything in the nature of a disaster could possibly threaten us. And now to find that over in England they were offering up prayers for our safety, as though we were an army of doomed ! We couldn't believe it. Moreover, we didn't believe it. Not just then, at any rate.

After lunch the C.P.O., the G.P.O.'s and the Troop sergeant-majors were summoned to meet the Major at a rendezvous two miles ahead. The rest of us took the chance of a snooze in the beautiful afternoon in the shade of the apple-trees. And so peaceful and idyllic were our immediate surroundings that it was quite easy to laugh at the idea that we were in such deadly peril as to need praying for. Later on the sergeant-majors returned with messages to the Troop-Commanders to take up the guns to their positions. Off went the Troops headed by a sergeant-major on a motor-cycle, who led them over a twisting lane through open cultivated fields. All the gun positions were in an area half a mile square, each in or near a farmhouse or barn, it being absolutely essential to have overhead cover against the incessant activity of the German reconnaissance planes. The guns were unhooked, put on their line ready for action, and the gunners commenced digging the pits, raising ramparts of earth which they revetted with anything useful that came to hand, old doors, corrugated iron, stakes, and fragments of brick walls.

The position was a mile south of Vlamertinghe. The Hooker was observing from an O.P. ahead, and soon the guns roared out, firing at the enemy over the top of Ypres which still remained in British hands. All the while waves of bombers were arriving to bomb Vlamertinghe, only a mile away, and the smoke from the explosions ascended into the blue sky in voluminous grey billows.

I walked over to the Battery Command Post to see the Major. As I entered he was in the act of putting his lips to a cup of tea. He paused, looked at me, and over the edge of the cup, in a voice just as casual as he might have used to observe that it was a fine day, said :

" The Belgians have packed up."

Astounding news. I could not believe it. My expression must have been a comic study, for the Major, as though taking a quiet delight in watching for a still further intensification of my amazement, added :

" They've laid down their arms. I've just heard it from R.H.Q. Have a cup of tea ? "

" Thanks. I will, after that pleasant bit of news."

I began to think that perhaps that National Day of Prayer might have had more justification than we in Y–Battery had imagined.

" The Third Division are coming in on our left in place of the Belgians," added the Major. " Thank God we have British Divisions now on each of our flanks."

Yes, that was a comforting thought. For the first time since the fighting began we could now feel that both our flanks were safe.

" We'll probably have to fall back again in order to shorten the line," continued the Major, calmly sipping his tea.

Pregnant words, these. They might mean anything. My thoughts flew off to the A.C.P.O.'s prophecy at Fresnoy that Boyd and I had laughed to scorn. But still there was no breath of evacuation—or Dunkirk. That name was yet to appear on the map of our future.

I walked back to M-Troop's position, where Ritchie, the G.P.O., had his Command Post in the cellar of a farmhouse with a grating just above ground level, through which he could bawl orders. On my way I noticed a lot of bits of paper fluttering down from the sky. Some of them drifted down into a field close by, and I crossed over and retrieved one.

A third surprise for the day. It was a German propaganda leaflet dropped by some aeroplane. It contained two statements, one printed in English, the other in French.

The former read as follows :

> " You are surround.
> The match is ended.
> Throw down your arms.
> We take prisoners."

To the French the mode of approach was somewhat different :

> " Your leaders have already fled by 'plane.
> Your country is in ruins.
> Throw down your arms."

One could not but admire the ingenuity of the mind behind these productions. They had been so carefully worded with a view to the different psychology of the two nations. The reference to the match being over, as intended to appeal to a people of sporting instincts, was a perfect gem. With the French a harder, more realistic line was taken. No pleasant, friendly suggestions to look upon themselves merely as the losing side in a Cup Final.

I don't know what the effect of that leaflet was upon the French. But I shall not go far wrong in presuming that with the B.E.F. generally the result was much the same as with Y-Battery. The men roared with laughter, and thought it the best joke for years. " The match is ended " especially tickled them.

" Ended ? Ended ? " cried one of the gunners. " Why, what *is* he talking about ? We've only just had the kick-off."

The best comment of the lot was uttered by a sergeant who, after reading the leaflet very carefully two or three times, said to me quite seriously :

" They must be in a bad way, sir, to descend to that sort of thing."

I wish Hitler could have been at hand to hear that sergeant. It would have given him many second thoughts on his preconceived ideas of British psychology —and possibly of other things British, too.

Anyhow, he'd have learned in an instant that " the match " was very far indeed from being " ended."

XIII—WE JOIN THE REARGUARD

Throughout that night and the following day our guns continued shelling the enemy on the far side of Ypres. On our side there was hardly an hour's relief from the bombers. They came over in schools, not from in front of us, but from our right rear, which made it a little more uncomfortable. The Germans had captured Cassel, which stands on a mound and provides an interrupted view for miles and miles over the flat plain. They had also taken possession of Mount Kemmel, which we could easily see from our positions. So there wasn't any doubt but that they could spot our gun-flashes.

About 4 p.m. I went to the Battery Command Post. The Major was in the act of telephoning down to the gun positions :

" Prepare to withdraw."

He replaced the telephone and began to speak to me. And from his words I obtained for the first time an inkling that the A.C.P.O. had been right all along. We were going to be evacuated to England.

" I want you to go along the road towards Vlamertinghe," he said. " You'll find another gunner regiment there, on the right. They are destroying their guns, and they have been ordered to give us two of their tractors to replace the two we've lost."

Destroying their guns ! The worst that can happen to a gunner ! There couldn't be any further doubt concerning the critical nature of the situation.

I hurried off, picked up a couple of spare drivers

and drove down the road through a small, badly-bombed village. Here I encountered my first sign of the new phase of the battle . . . a battery of anti-aircraft guns that had been blown up by Royal Engineers. Their splayed shredded muzzles—like great sticks of celery—looked oddly pathetic.

" Have you two tractors for me ? " I asked the Adjutant of the gunner regiment when I at last ran him to earth.

" Not heard anything about it," he replied. " Must be the other battery, farther on."

I combed the district for miles after that battery, but couldn't find them. Apparently they had pulled out, leaving a great bonfire of stores and material by the side of a bombed farmhouse. Higher up the road I ran across an anti-tank gun coming into action. The arrival of the German tanks was expected at any moment, so I gave it up and hastened back to the Battery.

We waited until dark before moving. Then the guns were hooked in and we journeyed under cover of night to the village of Oostuleteren, outside which we halted for an hour before going into the positions that had been picked for the guns by a regimental party that had proceeded in advance during daylight.

Dawn was just breaking as we settled in. All the positions were in farms except M–Troop's, which was sheltered behind a hedge containing trees. In front was a field, and a small farmhouse overlooked the field. Our sudden arrival here, in the still hours of the morning, created consternation among the occupants—an old peasant, his wrinkled wife and his two fat elderly daughters. We urged them to quit, giving gruesome imitations of the row the guns would kick up. But dazed and terrified as they were, they refused to budge. While we sat in the farmhouse shouting orders to the Troop, they plodded on with their

farm and household duties. This had one advantage.
For two or three days we had been without bread.
I invited the old woman to bake some for us. She
baked fourteen large loaves, for which I paid her
fifty French francs.

The disadvantage was that the farmhouse only contained one very small cellar. When an air raid
occurred the family completely monopolised it, leaving
no room for us. We had to remain above. Certainly
they didn't appear to care in the slightest what
happened to us.

The big field in front of the position stretched away
to a road running parallel to the line of guns and
leading to a little hamlet. We had not fired more
than a few rounds when the hamlet came in for a
severe bombing. Besides bombs there descended on
us more leaflets. One of them was brought to me by
Ritchie's G.P.O. Ack. It was a map showing Belgium,
Holland and France. The whole of this was dotted
with black swastikas except for the tiny bit of territory
jutting out from Dunkirk still occupied by the British
troops. All the place-names were put in. It was
really terribly up to date. A smart bit of work. And
looking at that tiny zone surrounded by the vast rest
of the three countries all covered with swastikas, you
could easily feel a trifle isolated. Certainly a far
better bit of propaganda than the " match has ended."

A French horse artillery regiment appeared, walking
along the road towards the hamlet that had just been
bombed. Suddenly a bomb burst close to the head
of the column. The effect was startling. Immediately
the column scattered in greatest confusion. One of
its wagons turned completely over. And before we
could say a word M–Troop, concealed behind the
hedge at the other side of the field, found itself in
the novel predicament of being about to receive a
cavalry charge. In a disorderly line, shouting and

yelling, the column dashed straight for the hidden
guns. On they pounded at top speed, drivers urging
and whipping up the horses on the limbered guns,
gunners clinging frantically to limbers, ammunition
trailers, mess-carts, G.S. wagons—all in one wild,
frenzied charge.

" This is magnificent, but it isn't war," said Ritchie.
" What are we going to do about it ? "

" Damned if I know," I replied. " There's nothing
in the Gunner's Handbook about this."

We could, in fact, do nothing but wait, fascinated,
and see what would happen. In the excitement of
the moment some of our gunners began to cheer.

And just as the leaders were about twenty yards
away, and a crash appeared inevitable, they evidently
decided they couldn't leap the hedge. With a wonderful instantaneous swerve the whole flying column
passed away to the right.

" That would go down damn well at the Military
Tournament," was Ritchie's comment.

Towards mid-day we were bombed again, but they
did not get closer than fifty yards. Lunch was taken
round to the gun crews and they ate whenever there
was a quiet spell. Ritchie and I were having ours in
the Troop Command Post when the telephone rang.

" Captain —— wanted," said the operator to me.

It was the Major. And he had a thrill to deliver.

" Get prepared to fire on tanks," he said. " Some
have broken through and are approaching in your
direction. They'll be preceded by motor-cyclist
troops."

" Firing with open sights at last. Fine," said
Ritchie as we dashed from the Command Post to the
guns.

The gun crews were informed of the emergency and
told to keep strict look-out for the tanks, not only on
the road in front, but on the left flank, too. They

were also warned to be careful not to fire upon any of our own troops who might be withdrawing. The anti-tank rifles were re-sighted to give a better field of fire for the job. The Bren-guns were brought out and placed between the guns. All spare numbers were armed with rifles. The guns were reloaded with a special shell and full charge. Within five minutes our little composite force was ready.

Several minutes of breathless waiting passed. A tank attack at close quarters is no joke. We took it seriously enough, anyhow. The tension could be felt.

Suddenly round the far end of the road there came into sight the figures of three motor-cyclists.

" Here they come," I said to Ritchie, for I could distinguish with my naked eye that their helmets were neither British nor French style.

I raised my field-glasses to have a closer look, and then saw they were three French Don R's, who wear a crash-helmet very similar in pattern at a distance to the German helmet. The cyclists vanished down the road and we continued our " Stand to." It was half an hour before the telephone bell in the Troop Command Post rang again, and the Major shouted down :

" All right. Tanks have been driven off."

And a big sigh of relief went up from M–Troop.

Not long after I received another message. Would I report to the Battery Command Post.

The B.C.P. was in a farmhouse, some six hundred yards down the road. When I arrived I found the C.P.O., the A.C.P.O., and all the Troop-Commanders already present. One of the B.C.P. Staff went round handing each of us a new map-sheet. I took mine without paying very much attention. We were already up in the corner of our last sheet, so I had expected we'd soon get a new issue.

Suddenly, glancing down at it, I noticed that a great proportion of the new sheet was occupied by the sea. Another look showed me a strip of coast. And the principal name on this strip was Dunkirk. It was the first time the word had struck us with any particular significance.

We weren't long left in the dark as to the precise nature of that significance. The Major entered the room and addressed us in short abrupt phrases :

" Gentlemen, we are falling back on Dunkirk. A lot of regiments are going out of action now. They are going to be evacuated to England. We are to join the rearguard of the B.E.F. They will be troops from three Divisions. We are one of the four artillery regiments chosen."

It was an honour, undoubtedly. But for the moment most of us thought the news a bit depressing. We weren't carried away by any false heroics. A rearguard action covering the evacuation was going to be no picnic. We might as well resign ourselves.

" We shall at once withdraw and come into action again near Adinkerke," continued the Major. He turned to me : " You'll go on ahead at once with the A.C.P.O. to reconnoitre positions."

XIV—ALL ROADS LEAD TO DUNKIRK

Y–Battery pulled out at half-past four in the afternoon. We hadn't proceeded far when we were struck by what seemed, at first sight, an extraordinary phenomenon. The entire countryside was a-flutter with white. From every house in the villages, from church steeples, farms, cottages, from everywhere where people lived there flapped a white flag, and if not a real flag, a white table-cloth, sheet, towel, or handkerchief. They were, of course, the tokens of surrender which the inhabitants were in a great hurry to have on display by the time the Germans arrived. Most of the private houses were heavily shuttered. Here and there little knots of silent people stood by the wayside. But we all had the feeling that the vast majority were peeping at us from behind the shutters with mixed emotions. Relief that the tide of war was departing from their neighbourhood, mingled with apprehensions of what troubles the entry of the Germans would bring in its train.

Approaching the bridge over the canal we once more found ourselves in a main stream of military traffic, some French but mostly British. The road narrowed here, and to add to the confusion a truck full of poilus, who seemed to be in a panic to get away, insisted on trying to pass all the other vehicles on the road. They were blocking up the whole procession, and causing dangerous delays as aeroplanes could be heard overhead. Shouts of " Pull-in. Pull-in. . . Wait your turn. . . . What's your hurry ? . . ." came from the angry British troops, mingled with oaths and curses. But the poilus took no heed. They insisted on forcing a passage through. At last they endeavoured to pass my truck. I didn't waste any words. I leaped out, drew my revolver, and told the driver that if he did not get back in line instantly I'd shoot him. He pulled in.

A few moments later, thirty yards from the bridge, the threatened air attack developed. Three bombers swooped low over the bridge and dropped their bombs. They missed the bridge but hit the banks. As the bombers swooped, everyone leaped from the vehicles and scattered over the fields on each side of the road. I crouched in a ditch. A few yards away a French soldier and a little boy had taken refuge. A bomb exploded and a fragment of it sliced head-and-shoulders off both. When the bombs finished, the machine-gunning started, the Germans, from only a short distance up, emptying belt after belt of bullets upon the troops in the fields. That over, we resumed our journey and passed through the village of Houthem.

The face of the country-side had now undergone a complete change. Miles and miles of low-lying marshy fields stretched far as the eye could see, all cut up by a network of canals and highways at right-angles to each other. Each field was below canal level, so each had its own diminutive dyke running round it. There were few trees to be seen anywhere, save the pollard oaks bordering the dead-straight roads.

Into this pancake of a land it seemed as if the whole of the B.E.F. was pouring. Every road scoring the landscape was one thick mass of transport and troops, great long lines of them stretching back far to the eastern horizon, and all the lines converging towards the one focus—Dunkirk. Ambulances, lorries, trucks, Bren-gun carriers, artillery columns—everything except tanks—all crawling along those roads in well-defined lines over the flat, featureless country in the late afternoon sunshine, provided an impressive and memorable picture of two modern armies in retreat. Under their greyish camouflage paint they resembled from a distance slow-moving rivers of muddy-coloured lava from some far-off eruption.

It was now that I saw, for the first time, regiments in the doleful process of wrecking their equipment. New wireless sets, costing perhaps £20 apiece, were placed in rows in the fields, twenty in a row, some-times, while a soldier with a pick-axe proceeded up and down knocking them to pieces. Trucks were being dealt with just as drastically. Radiators and engines were smashed with sledgehammers ; tyres slashed and sawn after they had been deflated. Vehicles that were near the canals were finally pushed in. Some of the canals were choked with the wrecks, all piled on top of each other. There was more wreck than water.

Also, from this point you encountered another novel sight in this war-on-wheels . . . infantry marching on foot. Having destroyed their transport they had to walk the last ten miles to Dunkirk. This was the infantry due for immediate evacuation. Not the rearguard. They were allowed to use their transport up to a later point.

Now progress along the roads, filled with pedestrians, and dusk falling, became terribly slow. The troops marched in single file along each side of the road, weary, red-eyed, and dust-begrimed. But cheerful, and still able to shoot off a bit of characteristic repartee when the occasion arose.

Night was falling when we reached our destination, a large farmhouse, miles from anywhere. Behind was a large field bordered by tall trees, and this was to be our " hide." In front of the house waved the white flag of surrender. When the guns drew into the gate out rushed the old farmer who was living there with five grown-up daughters. In a great state of excitement he picked on Tops, N–Troop Commander, shouting away at the top of his voice, gesticulating frenziedly, and pointing to the white sheet hanging out of the window. He wanted us to go at once and leave him in peace. Had he not hoisted the white flag ? Had not the Belgians laid down their arms ? And much more.

Tops listened patiently to begin with, but got tired of the old man's vehemence after a time, and walked off saying :

" My advice to you is, take the washing in. It may rain to-night."

The Colonel himself had picked the positions for the Regiment, for by now we were closely linked up with our sister Z-Battery. When the guns arrived they were able to go direct into them without using the " hide."

As soon as the last Troop was despatched I went over to the Battery Command Post, in the cellar of another farm at the village of Moeres, between three and four miles from Adinkerke. The owners had not yet departed, but regarding us as birds of ill-omen they made immediate preparations to leave first thing in the morning. Besides being the B.C.P. we had one of the Troops in a barn at this farm. Indeed, in this area the entire six Troops of the Regiment were in barns and farmhouses, the only cover available.

XV—WINDMILL VERSUS CHURCH

Our O.P. was in a white windmill. It was startlingly conspicuous, but we had no choice. In that flat area there was nothing else available. It was a regimental O.P. to be used by both Y- and Z-Batteries. For the remainder of the night it was to be manned by Z-Battery, and also during the next twenty-four hours. When I arrived at the Command Post the Major said :

" You'll go up to relieve their man the day after."

Before snatching some sleep I made a tour of the farmyard to see how the gunners were progressing with the pits. There was no need now to urge them to dig, as had been the case when we were going into action for the first time at Aspelaere. They had learned in the interval that their lives depended on it. Picks and shovels never stopped. Mounds of earth grew visibly. Concrete posts were found to revett the pits. It was a great race against the coming of dawn. One gun had been drawn into a brick farm, and a hole knocked through the wall for the muzzle. The wall was then strengthened with earth and bricks. When it was finished it made one of the most safe and comfortable gun-pits I had ever seen.

Next morning, when it became light enough to take a look round, we received a decided shock. Yonder in the village of Bulscamp which was in enemy country, rose a steepled church completely overlooking us.

" My word. They'll be able to see us from there, all right," said the Major. " We must have that down at once."

He measured the switch, range, and angle of sight of

the church from the map and gave orders to N–Troop
to open fire on it.   I stood beside him and we gazed
in the direction of the offending church to watch the
result.   But it was unsatisfactory.   From where we
were stationed we could not see the shell bursts in the
village, and so did not know what corrections to give
to the guns to bring them on to the church.   The
Major turned to me :

"Hop in your truck and go to the O.P. and do the
shoot on the church from there," he said.

I drove over to the windmill and climbed to the top.
The large attic-like room was full of the windmill's
machinery, ponderous wooden cog-wheels of colossal
size, with a great spindle striking down through the
middle of them to the bottom of the mill.   These great
wheels would start to revolve and creak when the
outside vanes were set in motion by the wind.   But now
they had been locked.   Wheels, spindle, and wooden
walls were thickly covered with black grease, and the
smell was appropriate.

At first, in the dim light, I could detect no trace of
Z-Battery's O.P. officer.   Then I perceived him high
up in the open roof above my head, perched athwart
a thick greasy beam, peering out through a hole in
the timbers.   I gave him a hail.

"Hullo.   What are you doing here ? " he shouted
down.

"I've got to shoot down a church," I called back.

"Hold on a second, then.   I'll come down and you can
have my beam.   I can recommend it for comfort.   After a
few minutes you won't know you've got a backside."

"Can I use your Ack ? "

"Yes, that's all right.   You can use anything of mine,
seeing the love I bear you for getting me off that beam."

I climbed up and took his place.   The warmth of
his body had melted the hard grease where he had
been sitting.

Through the hole in the timbers I took a view of the prospect. In the morning sunshine the country-side lay for miles before me, vivid and distinct. Immediately in front I looked across a series of flat green fields which were neatly bisected by a yellow road running direct into enemy country. In the middle distance I picked out groups of red farms, small clumps of osiers, and a level-crossing with a " Halt." Far away to the left the sunshine glistened on Furnes, as yet unsmashed by the bombers. To the right, in the far middle distance was Bulscamp just on the other side of the canal that the rearguard of the B.E.F. was holding as a line.

And in the centre of Bulscamp, from the middle of a cluster of red houses, rose my destined victim, a grey church with a tower surmounted by a wooden steeple. At once I fastened on the two slit windows in the belfry just below, visible from where I watched as little more than two short vertical lines. From these windows we, in our turn, were doubtless being observed by some German O.P. officer.

Just as the white windmill was our only possible O.P. so the grey church of Bulscamp was the German's. Windmill and church stood up facing one another over that flat stretch of land, like a couple of sharp exclamation marks. One British, the other German. It was going to be a duel. Windmill v. Church. And the result would largely depend on minutes. Seconds, perhaps.

I wasted no more time. As soon as I had measured the switch, range, and angle of sight to the church I sent them down to the guns, and the order to fire.

" Shot One, sir," announced my telephonist after a pause.

I raised my glasses to see the effect of the bursting shell. There it was. A wisp of whitish smoke rising from behind some houses on the left of Bulscamp.

" More Two Degrees," I ordered.

My next round fell, as far as I could estimate, just in front of the church. It was a lovely morning for observation. In the clear sunshine, with no trace of a haze, nothing could be missed.

I bracketed the church, and went on to fire for effect.

" One Round Gun-fire," I ordered.

" Shot," announced the operator at the end of ten seconds.

Up went my glasses and I saw the shells go tearing through the roof of the church.

I sent down a correction.

" More Ten-minutes. . . . Raise angle of sight Five Degrees. . . . One Round Gun-fire. . . ."

This time I had the satisfaction of seeing two of the four shells crash into the windows at the top of the belfry. Great lumps of masonry began falling.

" Good shooting," said the Z-Battery officer who had climbed up again to have a look.

But I was not entirely satisfied. So I got the Troop to send over another five rounds gun-fire to make positive that the Germans could not use that belfry again. Then I switched off the church and shelled the village for a bit. In a few moments great clouds of black, grey, and white smoke filled the air, mingled with dashes of red dust from the powdered tiles.

A good hour's work. I handed over to Z-Battery O.P. officer again.

" See you to-morrow at dawn," I said, and returned to the Battery.

The Major was delighted. He and the A.C.P.O. congratulated me heartily.

" Jolly good shoot," he said. " We had a fine view from here. We could see them hitting the tower. Quite exciting."

Sweet-sounding words, these, from such a fine gunner as the Major.

190

XVI—The Spitfires Show Up

" We're due for a bit of excitement," said the A.C.P.O. that afternoon.

" Haven't we had any yet ? " I laughed.

" A hundred Spitfires are going to fly over us," he continued.

" What ? " I yelled, incredulous.

Remarkable as it may sound, Y–Battery during all its wanderings from Brussels down to Arras, and back to where we now were, had not been vouchsafed a single glimpse of an air fight. We had seen Germans brought down by our ack-ack fire, but never by any Allied planes. So far as we were concerned the sky was theirs, and we had to make the best of it.

I recalled that drop of bitter humour squeezed from one of our gunners at Givenchy under pressure of savage dive-bombing :

" And to think I once paid a shilling to see the Hendon Air Pageant ! "

That summed it all up. Hence my incredulity on this occasion.

" A fact," insisted the A.C.P.O. " We've just had it from R.H.Q."

Shortly after, a large German bomber formation flew over our positions. We prepared for the usual heavy rain. Suddenly the sky changed. Down from heaven dropped a squadron of Spitfires, and also a number of Messerschmitt fighters. Within the twinkling of an eye we became sightseers of a grand battle. Almost immediately the German formation was broken up A Spitfire sent one bomber crashing to the

ground, while the occupants baled out. Dog-fights
commenced all over the sky. The air resounded with
the incessant rat-tat-tat of machine-guns. In a few
moments seven German parachutes were floating
slowly down at the same time. Five German planes
crashed in flames. A Spitfire drew out of the battle,
circling and losing height, black smoke pouring from
its tail. The only British loss, so far as I could see.

Y–Battery gazed on the battle with an excitement
growing hotter each second. It was their first glimpse
of our fighters in action since leaving Ninove, three
weeks before. And it was appreciated !

" Now you *are* here, show us what you can do ? "
yelled the gunners to the skies.

Cheer mounted upon cheer as the Spitfires cut the
Germans to ribbons.

" Another cokernut ! " was the favourite çry whenever an enemy plane crashed.

It was all over in a quarter of an hour. But what
a quarter ! Like a revelation of a better world for us,
after the long succession of days of unrelieved perse-
cution from above. Yes, the most heartening quarter
of an hour in Y–Battery's calendar for ages.

And for the time being the sky was ours. Marvellous. . . .

The A.C.P.O. was jubilant. It might have been his
own show.

" Does your old friend ever lead you astray ? " he
demanded proudly, as we retraced our footsteps to
the Command Post. " Didn't I prophesy we'd go
back to England ? Didn't I say the Spitfires were
coming ? "

" I don't think much of that as a bit of crystal-
gazing," I demurred. " All you did was to take a
message over the phone from R.H.Q. I could have
done as much myself. But I won't appear niggardly.
What's the next surprise in store for us ? "

" Oh, nothing more to-day.   Nothing more to-day,"
he replied airily.

And let this be a warning to soothsayers that it
is just as risky to forecast nothing as something.
When we entered the Command Post the telephone
bell rang.   The A.C.P.O. picked it up.   It was R.H.Q.
again.

" Will you take this message ?   From His Majesty
the King to . . . blocks on, ' C ' . . . blocks off, ' in '
. . . blocks   on,   ' C . . . B.E.F.' . . . blocks   off
(" blocks " indicated block letters).

" Message begins . . . ' All your countrymen have
been following . . .' "

The A.C.P.O. wrote the words down carefully and
repeated.

" Correct," said R.H.Q., and continued :   " ' with
pride and admiration the courageous resistance of the
British Expeditionary Force . . .' "

Again the A.C.P.O. repeats back.

" Correct . . . ' during the continuous fighting of
the last fortnight . . .' "

Another repeat.

" Correct. . . . ' Placed by circumstances outside
their control in a position of extreme difficulty . . .'

" Correct . . . ' they are displaying a gallantry that
has never been surpassed in the annals of the British
Army . . .'

" Correct . . . ' The hearts of everyone of us at
home are with you and your magnificent troops in
this hour of peril. . . .' "

Again the A.C.P.O. repeated back.

" Wrong. . . . Not ' pall.' . . . Peril . . . P for Pip
. . . E for Eddy . . . R for Robert . . . I for Ink
. . . L for London. . . .' "

" Peril," repeats the A.C.P.O.

" Correct. . . . Message ends."

" Hour of peril, eh ? " said the A.C.P.O. thoughtfully,

turning towards me. " Sounds pleasant, doesn't it ? I'd better send this down to the Troops."

He transmitted it over the telephone to the Troop Command Posts, where it was duly delivered to the gun crews.

That is how the King's celebrated message of good cheer reached Y–Battery while the guns were roaring out. The reception was typical. All the men thought it was exceedingly kind and thoughtful of the King to send them a few nice words. They appreciated it very much. But it really wasn't necessary. " Hour of peril ? " Oh, no, things were not so bad as that. A bit tough, perhaps. And it would be a bit tougher now they were in the rearguard. But nothing to get seriously alarmed about, personally. They utterly persisted in refusing to believe they were in any grave danger. Their confidence in themselves was sublime.

A quarter of an hour later the A.C.P.O. had a similar duty to perform. This time it was the Commander-in-Chief's reply to the King's message.

" The Commander-in-Chief, with humble duty, begs leave on behalf of all ranks of the British Expeditionary Force to thank Your Majesty for your message. May I assure Your Majesty that the Army is doing all in its power to live up to its proud traditions and is immensely encouraged at this critical moment by the words of Your Majesty's telegram."

Again, it was not the words " critical moment " that Y–Battery seized on, but the phrase " proud traditions." That they did understand, and realise vividly. Tradition was strong throughout the Regiment. There was a strong " family affair " flavour in the ranks. Sons joined the Regiment because their fathers had served in it before them. We had fathers and sons serving together now. And in at least one case, a father and two sons. Many of the gunners and drivers knew the history of the Regiment back to 1860. And all of them could reel off the long list of battles it had taken part in during the war of 1914–1918 : Ypres, Loos, the Scarpe, the Somme, Paschendaele, and others.

Finally the Adjutant rang up in the same vein.

"Hello, hello," he commenced with a boyish exuberance. "The Battle of All Time is about to begin. Probably shan't get back. Jolly good show, chaps. Jolly good show."

But by this time the A.C.P.O. was getting tired of the heroic.

"What the hell do you mean ? . . . Jolly good show ! " he replied, shortly.

He turned to me. "Good God ! What rot ! Fancy ringing up to tell me that."

*   *   *   *   *

Entering the Mess at tea-time after R.H.Q. conference, the Major said :

"From this position we shall probably have to march back on foot to Dunkirk. We must travel light. I advise you fellows to get rid of as much kit as possible."

"Yes. We'll do the last trip in our best clothes," said Tops. N–Troop Commander.

"Last trip to where ? " drawled the Babe.

No one answered him for a second or two.

"To dinner, to begin with," observed Tops, cheerfully.

"Followed by the Ride of the Best-Dressed Valkyries," laughed the Babe.

"That's an idea," interrupted the Major. "Let's have a really good dinner to-night. We mayn't get another for some time. Something we shall remember."

"Or be remembered by," added the Babe.

Tops departed to the cook-house to explain the

requirements. Such an important occasion demanded his personal domestic supervision.

"Now use your imagination," he exhorted the cooks. "And not all imagination, either. Some real food, too. What have we got?"

Meanwhile the rest of us disappeared to commence the mournful business of discarding our belongings.

I descended into the dark cellar that I shared with the Major, and which was lit by the stump of a guttering candle.

"Make two piles of the stuff on the bed," I said to my servant. "A little pile of what we can take, and a big pile of what we can't."

I said "we" at this momentous moment in unconscious recognition of the duality he had long assumed existed between us. My servant was a dark-haired, good-looking little Cockney who prided himself on his football prowess. But what impressed me more was his marvellous knack of "getting a girl" wherever we happened to be. Ten minutes was all the time he needed. The Battery had but to descend on a village and, if there were any presentable girls about, my servant in no time had discovered them and made choice of the one he was going to keep company with. It was sheer genius. Aided, of course, by his good looks.

As I have indicated, with me he was a dualist. With him it was not "you," but "we"; not "yours," but "ours." He had even reached the length of asking when he called me in the morning: "And how's our cough to-day, sir?"

"What about our shirts, sir?" he inquired now.

"I'll put on a clean one now," I replied. "Put that light shirt in the pack. Also a pair of clean pants, vest, towel, pyjamas, shaving-kit and tooth-brush."

I decided I'd make sure of my best tunic, for which

I had paid nine hundred francs in Lille only two months before, by wearing it. And the same with my best breeches, puttees and boots.

" What about our camera, sir ? "

" Shove it in the middle of the pack so that it won't get damaged."

What a flop that highly-expensive camera had been. I had brought it back to France from leave, largely at the pressing representations of my family, who panted for pictorial glimpses of the life I was leading. And I hadn't exposed a single film. When " pictures " did come along, I was far too busy with other things. to think of them.

Ah, yes. I must be sure and not forget to keep the extensive bullet-proof cigarette case that my sister had gone to so much last-minute trouble to buy for me as a parting gift when I first sailed for France. I removed it from my battle-dress blouse, and placed it in the breast-pocket of my tunic while I thought of it. It might come in handy yet.

" We ought to try to take our dress forage-cap, sir," said my servant.

All the books, novels, magazines, letters from home (scores of them treasured up for re-reading at odd intervals), artillery text-books and gun handbooks went into a heap for immediate destruction, along with my small but choice private medicine cabinet, full of cures for ills I had never caught. (Another family link.)

" Marvel how much stuff we have accumulated in a few months," observed my servant, studying the heaps on the bed. And I could hardly credit it myself.

" We haven't any cigarettes or tobacco left, sir, so we won't have to bother about them. Or the pipes. They can go."

This wasn't such good news as " our " tone endeavoured to imply.

At last the pack was complete.

" Put all that's left in the suit-case," I said. " Take everything and get as far as you can to England with them. If you have to jettison anything on the way throw the camp-bed away first. Next the suit-case. And last of all the pack. Try to get it home, or else back to me. But don't run any stupid risks trying to save it."

Then I took the armful of books, letters, and papers upstairs and made a bonfire of them under the back wall of the farmhouse.

While watching them burn, with a slightly melancholy interest, I heard a ping, followed by a tinkle of broken glass from the window behind me. Some Fifth Columnist, I thought. I'm being sniped. And just then another ping, and some more glass dropped hitting me on the neck. I waited no longer. I dashed for cover. A few minutes later, when I crawled out to investigate, I discovered to my shame that the sniper 'was none other than one of our own cooks engaged in knocking a hole in a window because his fire was smoking too vigorously.

I returned to the house, washed and shaved, changed from my battle-dress to my best clothes, and had the odd sensation that all I possessed in the world was what I stood up in. I wondered when I should take off those clothes again. Actually I never did till I was back in England.

As impromptu *maître d'hôtel* Tops had excelled himself. When we gathered in the mess at seven o'clock, so clean, shaven, and dressy that we felt quite proud of one another, there was the table covered with a 'spotless white cloth, illuminated by the light of a dozen candles (not in bottles but in real candle sticks) and further adorned by a handsome array of bottles of red and white wine. The mess servants had risen to the

occasion and were as spruce and tidied-up as we ourselves. By closing one eye, and perhaps half the other,
you could easily imagine (if you wanted to) that this
was a snug little dinner party, at the Berkeley, say,
and that the diners would be going on afterwards to
the theatre. Anyhow, it looked quite as much like
that as it did a bit of the rearguard of the B.E.F. in
their " hour of peril."

We preserved the illusion among ourselves by a tacit
understanding to refrain from conversation touch-
ing upon our immediate prospects. We gossiped
pleasantly about people we knew, went into anecdotes,
and praised the meal. How they had managed it,
heaven knows. Our food supplies had by now dwindled
down to the negligible. Yet the cooks produced as
the menu : Tomato soup, four roast chickens, potatoes,
peas, fruit salad, sardines on toast as a savoury, and
coffee.

And to crown it all the Babe passed round
Turkish cigarettes. That was a surprise. We were
under the impression that the Battery's last cigarette
had gone up in smoke days before. The Babe had also
hoarded a few of a very special brand of his own. Far
too precious to be applied to the lips of the profane.
While we enjoyed his Turkish, he regaled himself on
these dainty little things with their black paper and
gold tips. He smoked them out of a long black and
silver cigarette holder, his hand making graceful
movements as he manipulated it.

" Keep it up, Babe," laughed Tops. " It's just too,
too exotic."

The boom of the distant German guns, and the roar
of our own occasionally replying, furnished the orches-
tral accompaniment, and now and then reminded us
that all the time there was a fifty-fifty chance of a
shell extinguishing our candle-light. On the whole, it
was a cheerful but not boisterous party. There were

no songs. We never sang after leaving Houplin. All of us were tired so we broke up before ten.

" Better get to bed early," said the Major, rising from his chair. " We may have a hard day to-morrow. That was a damn fine meal. Tell the servants to congratulate the cooks. . . . Oh, and don't wake me unless there's anything urgent."

Like the rest of us, I went to sleep in my best clothes. Half-way through the night I was aroused by the guns suddenly thundering away outside my window. Someone had seen rockets go up and sent down the S O S signal. The guns had opened out on their S O S lines. But it was a false alarm. The firing died down again. I looked across at the slumbering Major. A second or two later I was in strong competition with him.

XVII—The Windmill Again

My servant shook me from my dreams.

" Pretty dark, isn't it ? " I muttered, suspicious lest he had been too punctual, and robbed me of another half-an-hour.

" Dawn just breaking, sir," he affirmed, shoving into my hand a mug of hot " gunfire."

Two mouthfuls of it, and I was wide awake. Which was " gunfire's " special virtue. I fastened on my boots and puttees, collected my map, binoculars and revolver, and departed for the white windmill.

The O.P. Officer from Z–Battery was still sitting on his beam when I arrived. He hastened down at my footstep.

" Here's the panorama, and the target record," he said. " I'm off."

He hadn't very far to go. His Troop was in position just underneath the windmill, and his bed awaited him in a cottage close-by.

" Don't speak to me," he implored, as I was about to say something. " You may wake me. I'm asleep already."

To-day I had my own telephonist, wireless operator and O.P. Ack. We settled down to make ourselves as comfortable as possible in the greasy loft, among all the windmill's cumbrous wooden machinery.

I swung myself up on to the beam and took a look through the peep-hole in the timbers. Again it was a beautiful morning, and every tree and house for miles stood out distinctly in the brilliant sunshine. Another lovely day for spotting. I saw the church at Bulscamp that I had shelled the morning before. Yes, I (and the Battery) had made a good job of that. It looked more of a ruin than I had expected, and the steeple had been completely sliced-off. Machine-gun firing was going on in the direction of the line by the canal which our rearguard was holding. Yonder to the left I looked towards Furnes. But the Furnes I saw was not the one I had left the previous morning. Instead of clustered roofs glistening in the morning sunshine, all that could be descried were flames shooting up in between the thinner folds of a thick curtain of smoke. The dive-bombers had dealt with it in the interval.

I took another glance through a slit in the wall behind me, and for the first time saw Dunkirk . . . Dunkirk that was to loom so tremendously in our lives within the next forty-eight hours. Again, there was nothing to be seen of the town. Dunkirk was just one great black low-hanging cloud in the western sky, stretching miles along the horizon, and at its stormiest centre appearing to bulge down till it swamped the earth. You could distinguish nothing. But there was an evil fascination about that big, ugly, threatening monster. Already I began to speculate on the unpromising mysteries concealed behind its mask. The stories of the slaughter on the beaches had not yet penetrated to our ears.

Our batteries continued firing on Bulscamp, and when any new promising target cropped up I sent it down to them. As the morning advanced the front line started springing to life. Truck loads of infantry and Bren-gun carriers sped down the yellow road traversing the flat fields, on their way towards the battle. Our gun-fire intensified and I watched the shells plunging into the heart of the village and causing tremendous havoc. Sometimes a Don R. detached himself from the green distance and tore down the road in our direction. After a little time the whole front became noisy with the crackle of heavy rifle fire. Then a group of farmhouses in the middle distance right in front of me, which the enemy were shelling, caught fire.

Two hours passed. Then, through my glasses I saw the distant fields dotted with little figures. It was our own infantry dribbling back in twos and threes.

" Get me the Colonel at R.H.Q.," I shouted to the telephonist. In a second or two he handed me the phone.

" The infantry are falling back to the line of the railway just in front of you," I announced.

" Thanks," said the Colonel. " Send down any more news as soon' as you can."

I kept my eyes on the little moving figures. They grew larger and larger. You could see now they were men.

Again I rang up the Colonel.

" They're coming right back beyond the railway. Only three-quarters of a mile in front of you now."

" Thanks. I'll see if I can find out something."

In a little while the telephone rang. It was the Colonel.

" We've lost some ground," he said. " We are going to counter-attack. Phone back if you see anything out of the ordinary."

What I did see was more and more truck-loads of infantry racing along the road towards the railway line. More Bren-gun carriers, too. Our own shelling grew hotter and hotter. Then after an hour, the little figures moved back no more. The counter-attack had been successful.

Not long afterwards the telephone rang again. It was R.H.Q.

" The enemy have crossed the canal to your right. They are advancing over open fields, we are informed. Can you see them ? "

By shoving my head and shoulders through some
broken timbers in the wall and staring hard, I managed
to distinguish the black dots that were the enemy's
advancing infantry.

" You can use it as a regimental target," said the
Colonel when I informed him.   Which meant that I
could fire the combined twenty-four guns of the two
batteries at it.

Soon I had ranged and got a shell in the area, and
immediately went to fire for effect.   It was an impressive sight when those twenty-four guns commenced firing rapid fire on the fields.   The shells
hailed down upon them, and the entire ground sprouted
with red-orange flashes.   Of the German flanking
movement I saw nothing more.   It was blotted from
view by the smoke.   For the time being it just
withered away.

Soon I had something unpleasantly pressing to
divert my attention.   German shells began to sail
past the windmill far too close to be comfortable.
They burst about a hundred yards behind, and on
each side.   From the size of the shell-holes I judged
I was being fired at by heavy calibre guns, something
in the 5.9-inch class.   Within a very short space of
time the shells were bursting only twenty yards from
the windmill.   It was pretty obvious that the enemy
knew we were using the windmill as an O.P. and had
determined on destroying it.   Just as the day before
I had destroyed their O.P. in the church.   It was
equally obvious from the manner in which their shells
crept nearer that it was probably only a matter of
seconds before we should be requiring a new O.P.
And also, very likely, a new O.P. officer.

I 'phoned to the Major, outlined the new position,
and warned him that we had better begin looking for
a new O.P.   In a short while the Colonel himself
rang me.

" You are to remain at the O.P., however bad things are," he said. " It is a justifiable risk, and necessary for the shooting of the battery."

That settled that. All I had to do was to wait for the smack.

Then a curious thing happened. The shelling suddenly stopped. Surely, I thought, they're not giving it up. They were not. After a pause the shells began to come over again, this time in a much more harassing fashion. Either the German gunners had lifted the angle of sight or altered the range. And now, high up on my perch in the rafters of the windmill loft, I could hear the shells swish-sh-sh, swish-sh-sh as they passed a yard or two over the top and round each side. They were so near that they sounded to be just whizzing past my ears. First one side, then the other. Every moment I expected the top of the windmill to go, and myself with it. It quivered like a startled animal as each shell flew by simply from the vibration set up in the air.

When this had lasted for a few minutes I became obsessed with the idea that I was being made the subject of a refined form of torture. So accurate were the German gunners in just shaving the top of the windmill without hitting it that I began to believe they were doing it on purpose. Playing with me, like a cat with a mouse. And when they were tired of the game they would blow me to smithereens. Also, I began to fancy they were having their revenge on me for the way I had treated their O.P officer in the church at Bulscamp the day before. This proved a most uncomfortable thought. Of all the different kinds of justice to which one can fall a victim poetic justice is the most distasteful. It is so right. And therefore so painful. I had quite a bad quarter of an hour sitting on that beam thinking of that German O.P officer the day before, with my shells bursting on him.

Incredible to narrate! They never hit the wind-mill after all. Though if the shells had been red-hot they'd have scorched it. When the excitement sim-mered down, and the near shelling ceased, I handed over the watch on the front line to my O.P.Ack and went downstairs for a rest. Also to draw a couple of deep breaths.

The Troop Commander and the G.P.O. said :

" After all that, come over to the Command Post and have a drink."

We each had a stiff whisky in the little cottage by the windmill and strolled out into the sunshine again. And again the shelling began. The Troop Com-mander and the G.P.O. had dug for their own use a tiny slit trench, four feet long, two feet wide and three feet deep. It was just large enough to shelter them if they sat one at each end with their knees drawn up. At the first shell burst they took a dive into their trench, leaving me' standing forlorn on the brink. I was too diffident to follow them. After all, it was their private trench, and obviously not meant for three. I couldn't very well gate-crash. I looked around for other cover, but there wasn't a hide to be seen. Then another shell burst close at hand, sprinkling me with earth, and, much to my relief, I heard a voice rising from the ground :

" Come in, old chap. See if you can find some room."

I went head first into the slit between their knees. I got my head in and my legs. But my hind quarters refused to be squeezed in ; they remained sticking up like a tight hump above the top of the trench, feeling painfully forlorn and exposed. At every shell burst, as the fragments flew over me, I found myself thinking : " Good God, am I going to have to stand up for the rest of my life ? "

There was a pretty white, red-roofed farmhouse with

green shutters about four hundred yards from the
O.P. I had noticed four holes in the wall, each twenty
yards away from the other, and concluded it was a
Z–Battery Troop position.

I climbed back to the beam in the windmill, and it
happened that the first thing my eyes rested on was
this white farmhouse. Suddenly, without the slightest
warning, a salvo of enemy shells landed slap on top
of it.

My first thought was a professional one. . . . What
a lovely salvo ! Where had it come from ? The farm
hadn't been ranged on at all. The shells simply
dropped from the blue like a thunderbolt. True, the
German gunners very often did fire without ranging,
or else ranged with salvoes. In any case this was a
very lucky hit. One in a thousand. And just as I
thought that, as if to contradict me, a second salvo
landed on exactly the same spot.

My brief second of admiration for the gunnery
vanished. I began wondering what damage the
Troop had suffered. It looked very nasty indeed.
Who among my friends were down there ? What
had been their fate ? Disturbing premonitions took
hold of me.

But a new development swept these out of my
mind. One company of a machine-gun battalion had
dug in on the embankment of the road just in front.
The Germans began shelling the area again very
severely. The Z–Battery Troop at the windmill below
me opened out with rapid fire. And at the same
moment the machine-gun company came into action.
The din was deafening. Up in the windmill loft we
couldn't hear one another speak without yelling at
the top of our voices. And it was in the height of this
pandemonium that my telegraph operator, trying to
send a message to the Battery, shouted in my ear :

" Line dead, sir."

Presumably it had been cut by the shell fire.

" Try R.H.Q.," I shouted back.

" Dead also," he reported after a few moments.

I tumbled off the beam and dashed downstairs to my truck.

" Get the Major at the Command Post," I roared to the wireless signaller, for down on the ground the noise was even worse than up in the windmill. I hung over him anxiously while he chanted :

" Robert Eddy calling X . . . Robert Eddy calling X. . . . Can you hear me ? . . . Can you hear me ? . . . If so, answer . . ."

Eventually it was the A.C.P.O. who answered. I could hear him, but the row going on outside the truck was so tremendous, what with the roar of the guns and the rattle of machine-gun fire, that he couldn't hear me.

" What's the matter ?   What's all that noise up there ?   Is it you shouting too much ? "

I repaid this amazing compliment to the power of my vocal chords by simply bellowing :

" Get the Major."   And at last he heard.

I informed the Major that the wires were broken and that I had no touch with R.H.Q.

" I'll see what I can find out," he said, and I was just about to go off the 'phone when the A.C.P.O. of Z–Battery dashed up on a motor-cycle.

" Hold on," I asked the Major.

The A.C.P.O. looked pretty upset.

" Ack-Troop in the farm has had a bad knock," he shouted to me above the din.   " The Major has been killed.   We have orders to pull out."

" Ack-Troop badly shelled.   Major —— killed. They've orders to pull out," I yelled back to our Major.

I felt the pause with which he received the news of this disaster.

" I'll get in touch with you in a few moments," he said.

While I waited I had one or two twinges over the fate of Z–Battery's Major. He was one of my oldest friends in the regiment. But as I have said before, this speed warfare gives one little time at the moment for indulging in reflections. Also, the shells were falling round us so thickly that I was expecting any second to meet mine.

The Major's voice again :

" Pack up and come in. The Battery is going out of action."

I raced upstairs, collected my two assistants and my stuff, and we tore down to the truck. Shells crashed about us as we drove off at top speed past the machine-gun company, who were still in action.

At the Command Post they were packing up to go. They, too, were being shelled in full.

" Quick. Have a cup of coffee," said the Major. " You've had a pretty hot time."

" One or two pieces, sir ? " said the Major's servant, without a shake in his voice, handing me a cup as a shell exploded just outside.

XVIII—THE RING ROUND DUNKIRK

Nobody had the slightest illusions about the situation. We had to get out quick, or be hit ourselves.
By now L–Troop's tractors had arrived at the Command Post and the guns were being hooked in. The
sergeants urged the gunners on to the last ounce of
energy and speed.

"Hook this bloody gun in! Don't play with
it . . ."

"I can see you want to stop one . . ."

"Come on, suicide . . ."

And many other dark and well-ornamented insinua-
tions that the men were dallying about because they
purposely wanted to get killed.

At last the Troop moved out with the Command
Post staff on to the road. Two hundred yards ahead
a couple of shells burst by the roadside and the smoke
drifted our way. There was a bad stretch in front of
us. For nearly a quarter of a mile the road was
under semi-observation by the enemy. Shells dropped
intermittently on each side. We speeded the vehicles
up, praying we should not encounter a traffic block.
All went well. We passed the danger spot safely,
breathed more freely and soon reached the outskirts
of Adinkerke. We passed through the village with
its modern-looking wideish streets, all now scored with
shell-holes and strewn with broken glass. Otherwise
Adinkerke did not appear to have been damaged very
much.

Turning left, we now travelled for a mile beside the
canal leading to Dunkirk. Here the road was packed

with troops on the last stage of the march to Dunkirk. The retreat had now developed into a vast hike. Thousands and thousands of men, walking in twos and threes towards the sea, terribly fatigued and worn and dusty, but calm, cheerful, and steady. Not the slightest sign of hurry, or panic. Not even of any pressing anxiety. It looked exactly like the end of a mammoth hike after a tiring hot day. Here was the British Army preserving its morale even after it had ceased to be an Army.

Though there was little semblance of order there was no disorder. Officers and men were all mixed up together. Different units were largely broken up into individuals or small groups. Many of the soldiers had cut down branches of trees and used them as walking sticks. Which further helped the illusion of a hike. They all wore their tin-hats and carried their rifles slung. Many of them also were laden with little bits of personal luggage (another touch of the hike). You gathered a curious impression from this spectacle of all these thousands of tramping, steady men. One rather in the nature of a paradox : That the British Army, though broken, remained unshaken. Such was the effect " put over " by all these strong, imperturbable, self-reliant faces. You could even fancy them a patriot army on the way to battle. So little did they manifest the signs of defeat and disaster on their fair ruddy countenances.

Through these plodding thousands of fatigued men, ambulances full of wounded threaded their slow way, the sides riddled with bullet holes and their windscreens shattered. Apart from this the only wheeled traffic now to be seen on the roads were motor-cyclists, French lorries, and the transport of the rearguard regiments going up to make the last stand round Dunkirk. The road ran through an almost unbroken double hedge of wrecked vehicles. On one side the canal was piled high with them ; on the other they stood in great heaps the whole length of the deep ditch. It was destruction upon such a vast scale, all these thousands of broken useless machines, that it exerted a depressing effect beyond even the power of all these unbroken men to dissipate entirely. On the canal side, half a mile away were humped the sandy, tufted dunes stretching away to the sea, which, however was not visible. And it was now that we saw for the first time the bombing of the beaches. The first wave of early evening bombers roared over us towards Dunkirk, two miles away. We watched them circle and dive. Then sounded the thud, thud of the explosions.

By now we weren't altogether unaware of what was happening on the beaches. Our progress along the road had been at a snail's pace. We went forward three or four yards, then made a forced halt sometimes lasting a quarter of an hour. It was during these halts that we picked up a very good idea of the horrors going on at Dunkirk from scraps of conversation with the infantry. These gave rise to scraps of uneasy conversation among ourselves.

" Have you heard that they're gunning 'em as well as bombing 'em ? . . ."

" Some have been on the beach three days before they got a boat. . . ."

" Got safely on the destroyer and it was bombed. Most of 'em blown to bits. . . ."

" Hundreds of dead and dying on the beaches. No chance for them at all. . . ."

" I've just been told that they gun the fellows as they are swimming to the lifeboats. . . ."

" What'll it be like when we get there ? . . ."

" Shall we get there ? . . ."

" What d'you think our chance is ? . . ."

" Evens. . . ."

" I put it just under. . . ."

It will be realised from these bits of talk among us that Y–Battery was having its eyes opened.

It was at one of these halts that I asked our saddler, who had been a gunner in the Mons retreat, how it compared with the present one. His view that Dunkirk was the worse.

" At Mons we always had the possibility of going forward again, sooner or later. Here we know we shan't. That's what makes it bad."

On the occasion of another halt the brother of the A.C.P.O. of Z–Battery narrated to me the details of the death of their Major in the German salvo that I had seen fall on the white farmhouse. A–Troop and the Battery Command Post were established in the same house, the Command Post in a cellar. Their first realisation of having been spotted was the arrival of the salvo I had witnessed. Two shells landed in two of the gun-pits, killing and wounding most of the gun-crews. Another went through the door and down the steps into the cellar, killing the Major's driver, wireless operator, and servant, and blowing half the Major's right leg off. He crawled across the cellar, dragged himself up the steps to the farmyard, and started to shout encouragement to the remainder of the Troop. Another shell burst right in front of him. He collapsed, and never moved again.

A gallant death. Just what anyone knowing the man would expect. Z–Battery was very much affected by the loss of their popular Major. I had to grieve for a friend of twelve years' standing. He was a fine, courageous, great-hearted man. Dark, handsome, and six-feet-five in height. A solicitor by profession, thirty years old, and famous as a mountain climber. When I first joined the regiment he was senior subaltern. His death cut short the career of a fine soldier, and a fine friend.

Another flock of bombers now appeared on their way to hammer the ruins of Dunkirk to a still greater degree of devastation. It was seven o'clock. The great pall of smoke spread wide a hundred feet over the town like Death's hovering wing. Underneath, the tops of the tall skeletons of wrecked buildings and churches were silhouetted in black against the strip of pure lilac evening sky sandwiched between the horizon and the lower edge of the dark, threatening wing. Amidst these silhouettes huge fires raged, the long tongues of orange flame leaping high into the air as if in an angry endeavour to singe the thick, oppressive plumes of that wing.

It was a very forbidding spectacle. Looked at as a refuge, a sanctuary, a gate of escape, it was anything but inviting. We seemed to be heading straight for a holocaust ; far worse than anything we had witnessed so far. You had the impression that the last ordeal awaiting you was " ordeal by fire." It was a picture that reduced one to silence.

The German 'planes, about forty big two-engined bombers, flew on steadily in formation. They appeared to be approaching the direction of the road. If so we were for it. They couldn't miss the target of the crawling column inextricably mixed up with all these thousands of foot-slogging, weary troops. Already there were big bomb craters lining the sides of the road, showing us it had not escaped attention on previous occasions. A mad rush for cover started. Men packed themselves into ditches, crawled underneath the wreckage of vehicles, flattened themselves down between the very grass blades in the fields, and stood up to their necks in the water of the canal. In the space of a few seconds the mass of humanity that had encumbered the road had utterly vanished. Not a soul was in sight.

Yes, one—Y–Battery's saddler. At the moment

the dive for safety began he happened to be looking at some French Army horses that had been turned adrift in a field.   He noticed that one of them had become entangled in some barbed wire.   Without paying the slightest heed to the approaching bombers, or to his own safety, he calmly walked across the field with a pair of wire-cutters.   On reaching the nervous captive he commenced to soothe and pet it, taking his time, quite unruffled, just as he might have behaved outside a loose horse-box in the quiet heart of Leicestershire.   When the scared animal had quietened the saddler stooped down and began to cut away the barbed wire entangling its legs.   Then, with a friendly pat on its rump and an " Off you go," he walked back across the field, turning once or twice to glance smilingly at the horse as it trotted about, happy in its new-found freedom.

It was a striking display of cool nerve.   But even more striking was this quiet act of humanity suddenly blossoming, as it were, in the middle of the moment when inhumanity was flinging its shadow over the earth from the skies.

The saddler had no need to make a belated search for cover.   The bombers had swerved away from us and were now raining their bombs on Dunkirk.

The Battery continued its tedious progress for another half a mile along the road, when we were halted by a gunner, one of our own guides, who directed us down a side road to the left.   It was now getting dusk.   A hot night succeeding a hot day.   All of us were tired, thirsty and coated with dust which clogged our nostrils and throats.   A mile and a half from Rosendaal the Major appeared, like us, dusty and worn out.

" We are going into action three-quarters of a· mile down the road on the right," he said.

The narrow pavé road led through dead-flat green

grass fields, spreading on either side of us as far as
the eye could see. In the dusk it was a particularly
uninspiring landscape. There were no hedges, and
long ditches cut up the fields. Into one of these
fields we deployed, and a remarkable scene awaited
us. The four gunner regiments comprising the rearguard artillery that were to support the infantry
battalions in the last stand at Dunkirk were all start-
ing to draw up in position. They were forming a
wide ring of guns round Dunkirk, somewhat in the
rough shape of a three-sided square, the fourth side
being the Dunkirk beaches. It looked very much
like an old-fashioned battlefield of the cannon-ball
era—Inkerman, say—with the guns drawn up in a
hollow square.

The sides of this rough square faced east, north
and south. Y–Battery came into position on the north
side. On our left another gunner regiment carried
on the line of guns away into the sand dunes, practically
to the sea. Our twin sister, Z–Battery, was round
the corner, their guns pointing eastwards. Altogether
the four regiments hemmed in Dunkirk on the three
land sides about a mile from the outskirts of the
town.

A lorry ablaze behind one of the other batteries
lit up the dusk. Stragglers still dribbled down the
road past us, on the north by the side of the canal.
But not many of them. They became fewer and
fewer because, except for the battalions of rearguard
infantry holding the vague line a mile or so in front
of us, we were the last troops to fall back. It was
a ragged front line. On the north the French had
opened the sluice gates and flooded a certain amount
of low-lying ground. This in places slowed up the
enemy advance. Here and there our infantry were
separated from the enemy by wide stretches of water,
which, although not deep, was sufficient to slow up

the tanks. On the north side we hadn't them to fear, which was one comfort.

What was not so comforting was the complete absence of cover in these bare, flat fields. There was not a single bush or barn to conceal a gun. We were going to feel very naked and exposed when daylight came.

The Major had a brain-wave in the direction of camouflage.

" We won't send the staff vehicles (eight hundred-weight and fifteen hundredweight trucks) to the Wagon Lines," he said. " We'll keep 'em and dot 'em all over the field behind us. The Germans may think it is just another lot of abandoned vehicles, and it will serve as camouflage for the guns."

So while the gun-tractors and ammunition trailers went off to the Wagon Lines in a brickfield on the outskirts of Dunkirk, the trucks were strewn over the field in as disorderly fashion as possible, fifty yards behind the guns.

Two yards behind the line of guns ran a fairly deep dry ditch. This was used as a slit trench for the protection of the gunners. The Battery Command Post was established at the junction of this ditch and another, some thirty yards away, in prolongation of the line of guns. Over it we hoisted a bit of green tarpaulin.

That was all that could be done in the way of protection and cover on this naked plain.

" Do you want to see home again ? "

" Yes, sir."

" Then dig like hell."

The men wanted no further incentive. They dug as though their lives depended on each spadeful. Which, indeed, was the case. They dug so fast that you could almost see the guns sinking into the ground. By now it was pitch dark, and there was no sound but the noise of the digging.   Officers and men together, stripped to the waist.

It was midnight when the guns commenced firing. We had no O.P. and were firing at targets picked off the map, sending our shells crashing into the Germans advancing on Adinkerke.   The scene now developed a grim grandeur of its own.   A mile behind us, Dunkirk, as the darkness of the night closed in on it, ceased to be visible as a vast welter of black-and-grey smoke and became a great red, angry, glowing cinder.   The pillar of cloud by day became the pillar of fire by night.   Against the impenetrable ebony background of the sky it glared forth upon us like a ferocious bloodshot eye.   In front, along the near horizon, a couple or so miles distant, long flashes like summer lightning played continually, orange and greenish in hue.   They were the explosions of our own shells mingled with the flashes from the German artillery replying.   Above this play of summer lightning, every now and then a rocket soared high into the sky, bursting into a brilliant white light.   German success rockets recording the capture of some objective. They were disconcerting to watch, bursting as they did with such frequency, and in the darkness seeming to draw nearer and nearer.   I experienced the same uncomfortable sensation that had been mine that night alone on top of Vimy Ridge when I had felt the success rockets to be encircling me.

Lastly, between the glare of Dunkirk behind and the coloured lightnings of the eastern horizon, the great tongues of flame, two or three yards long, that leaped out into the darkness from the muzzles of the guns of our own and all the other batteries in the rearguard.   They lit us up with their continual lightning flashes.   The earth shook under the thunder of the explosions, which at times completely drowned the distant boom of the enemy fire.

Suddenly, from close out at sea came a terrific whitish flash followed by a roar passing over our heads that resembled a Tube train grating and rattling through a tunnel. It was a fifteen-inch shell from H.M.S. *Rodney*, which was shelling Ypres, fifteen miles away.

Boyd emerged from the darkness and touched me on the elbow.

" Doesn't it sound comforting," he said fervently. " The Navy is out there looking after us. That means we've still got a chance."

" Yes," I replied, with a glance back at fiery, forbidding Dunkirk. " We have—if, when our turn comes to go to the beaches it's at night. And if we don't have to wait long."

Boyd followed my look.

" No, it doesn't look very healthy," he murmured, a bit subdued.

Y–Battery was still digging and firing alternately. At one a.m. containers of stew and dixies of tea were brought up to the ditch by the cooks, and the detachments that were digging broke off for a few mouthfuls.

Sleep, as it is known, was an impossibility. A stretch of ten unbroken minutes was a luxury that few attained. We took it in turns to lie down in the bottom of the ditch . . . in our best clothes.

My best breeches already displayed a gaping rent at the right knee.

XIX—LAST HOURS

Dawn. . . . The Glorious First of June. . . .

Over there in front of us, German-wards, the horizon whitens. It is a pale, steady dawn, breaking with a slight haze that presages another scorching day. Whatever is to be our fate, we are evidently going to have a fine day for it. Behind us the red fires of Dunkirk fade to orange in the gathering light, thinning till they are no longer visible, and Dunkirk resumes its daytime hue, unrelieved funereal black.

The firing slackens down. But the day is not for long to make its debut in comparative quietness. Roaring from out of the brightening horizon, racing the sunrise, comes the first wave of bombers on their way to inaugurate another day of Dunkirk's purgatory.

On the outskirts of the town, half a mile behind us over the flat fields, stands a large factory. A French regiment is bivouacking there. The German bombers single it out for the commencement of their morning's work. I see the planes dive like hawks, and a rain of bombs drop. Huge pillars of smoke ascend.

Suddenly one corner of the factory blows up with an explosion that rocks the earth. Lumps of brick and masonry are hurled hundreds of feet in all directions. Brilliant flashes like magnesium flares illuminate the black heart of the wreathing smoke. Orange, blue, reddish, yellow flashes.

Boom . . . Boom . . . Boom . . . at very short intervals. More explosions. The bombers have hit an ammunition dump.

Then, mingled with these explosions, the roar of our own guns as they come into action again. . . .

*   *   *   *   *

Ten o'clock.   Another wave of bombers. . . .

These pay no more attention to the factory.   They concentrate on the beaches, bombing and machine-gunning the worn-out, exhausted troops.   This time their visit coincides with the visit of our own fighter planes.   Another fierce air battle develops over Dunkirk and spreads back to our own positions.

We break our necks, looking above the tops of our heads. . . .

A French fighter is attacking a big German bomber. He swoops, fires, climbs, circles, dives, fires again in thrilling style.   The bomber is worried, but apparently not mortally hit.   More German fighters appear. . . . The air fills with puffs of smoke as the Bofors shells burst round them.

Our eyes stare.   We catch our breath. . . . Without any warning the Frenchman has suddenly driven his machine head-on at the German at a terrific pace. They meet with a crash that echoes in the sky.   For the briefest second the two machines hang suspended in the air above our heads, locked in the death embrace. Then the engine of the bomber is seen to shoot out of the wreck in one direction and come hurtling to the ground.   A wing drops off.   Then another. . . . Bits of fuselage rain down on our battery positions.

Before the mass of wreckage falls two Germans jump from it in parachutes.   They float down some little way in front of us.   There is no sign of the heroic Frenchman who made sure of victory, and death, in one and the same instant.

Both the Germans are shot before reaching the ground by some French troops. . .

We cannot feel pity for them.   No one could, after

watching those waves of merciless bombers diving
down upon the Dunkirk beaches, hour after hour
throughout the livelong day. No one could, who
knew their ghastly errand. . . .

*   *   *   *   *

After this, incessant waves of bombers, hour after
hour, thirty at a time. A monotonous errand of
death. . . . Rather appalling by its sheer mechanical
precision. Not men doing it, but live machines.
Ruthless, soulless. . . . So one can imagine. . . .

Whether men, or machines, or both, they worked
like automata. The orders were to bomb the beaches,
and they carried them out to the letter, unless it
happened that our fighter patrol had arrived to greet
them. Beach-bombing was their job, and they stuck
to it with true German thoroughness. No deviations.
For instance, on their way to Dunkirk and back they
flew over our battery positions a score or more times.
They must have known we were there. Anybody
could see us on that flat open plain. Yet, save for
one rare occasion, they left us entirely alone. Not a
bomb. Dunkirk was the order.

The solitary exception happened at about eleven in
the morning, when a couple of dive bombers that had
already bombed the beaches decided, daringly, to
exceed instructions, and machine-gun our area. Everyone dashed for the ditch, lying flat in it while the
bullets hummed in the air. They gave us a bit of a
scare, and I hope they got severely told off for doing
so when they reached their 'drome !

*   *   *   *   *

Twelve o'clock. . . . The Major wants to see me at
the Command Post, otherwise, under the tarpaulin in
the ditch. Tops and the Hooker, the Troop Commanders, are already there.

" We will be blowing up our guns at ten-thirty to-night," says the Major.

Ten-thirty. . . . This, then, is our appointed zero hour. At half-past ten, if we still happen to be alive, we shall turn our faces at last towards Dunkirk, and march into that hidden fury of flame and smoke. What horrors shall we find there ?   Will they surpass those of Rumour and of our own imaginations ?   Will that fiery glowing cinder be our gate of escape ?   Can such a paradox happen ?   Or will it consume us as it has already consumed its thousands ? . . .

Anyhow, thank God we are going down to the beaches at night, and not in daylight !

The Major is addressing the Troop Commanders.

" See that by ten-thirty your guns are prepared for demolition," he says.   " All unnecessary personnel will be going back to the Wagon Lines at once, and will go down to the beaches early this evening for evacuation.   It is only necessary for one officer per Troop to stop."

He turns to the C.P.O. and the A.C.P.O.

" One of you can go," he says.

" We both prefer to stay," they reply.

The Hooker (suffering very badly from sore feet) and the Babe go from L–Troop, leaving the G.P.O. in charge.   Tops, N–Troop Commander, stays, and so does Boyd.   Ritchie goes, and so does the Wagon Lines Officer.   The Major, of course, stays.

*   *   *   *   *

Outside, the Troop Commanders are giving instructions to the Number Ones of the guns to detail all superfluous troops to start immediately for the Wagon Lines.   Five men only are to remain to man each gun.   There is no time to be lost.   The start is in ten minutes.   This matters not at all.   Nobody has any kit left to collect.   Nothing to speak of.

A slightly solemn air pervades the Battery. No one speaks much. Orders are carried out calmly and without any sign of bustle.

Nobody will accuse us of undue emotional tendencies if I remark that although words were few, we all had our thoughts. It was not to be expected that we should face the break-up of the Battery with indifference. For three hard weeks we had fought together, suffered together, escaped death daily together. Such links bind men tight. Quite apart, these, from the ties of friendship and respect formed during the long years before the war hit us. And at last we were to be divided. Some were to go, some were to stay. Henceforth our fates would be different. And no one could faintly foresee what each would be. The chances were that a good many of us would never see one another again.

*   *   *   *   *

The Number Ones have picked the men to stay, guided a good deal by physical condition. Anyone with the slightest suspicion of sore feet or muscle-strain goes. Most of the drivers, the batmen, and nearly all the signallers were already on their way across the field to the vehicles. The gunners are in the ditch putting on their battle-dress blouses and equipment, and collecting their few bits of stuff. Every man is issued with a tin of bully beef and a packet of biscuits, and ordered to guard it as he would his life.

" Understand, this is for when you get down to the beach. There'll be no possibility of getting any food there, and you may be held up there for some time."

In addition, they all have their iron rations, packed in a flat tin. Chocolate and meat extract of a food content lasting twenty-four hours

The ten minutes is up. The vehicles are all loaded, and off they go to the Wagon Lines *en route* for

Dunkirk.   A few quiet farewells. . . . A few shouts
of :
   " Good luck.   Good luck ! "
   " See you in England. . . ."
   They disappear, leaving fifty out of the Battery's
complement of two hundred and fifty behind.

*   *   *   *   *

The fire started in the factory just behind us by
the early-morning bombers has now assumed huge
proportions.   Evidently the flames have reached an
oil store.   Vast columns of black smoke are belched
up into the sky.   They spread out flat like a thick
dense cloud which slowly drifts over the Battery.
Soon the sun is completely obscured.   We are plunged
into mourning.   The gunners, at their work of loading
and firing, move like figures seen in the ghastly half-
light of an eclipse.   Boom. . . . Boom. . . . Still the
explosions of the shells in the ammunition dump
continue to shake the air.

*   *   *   *   *

Lunch . . . in the ditch under the tarpaulin.   The
sun once more is beating down on us with terrific
heat.   The Major, the C.P.O., the A.C.P.O., Boyd
and I have our lunch together.   Out of tins. . . . The
Major's servant has been rummaging in the officers'
mess-vehicle, which is one of those still dotted over
the field behind.   He manages to scrape together two
tins of Maconochie (stew), a tin of cold potatoes, already
cooked, a tin of Heinz beans, and some " issue biscuits,"
which are terribly hard, like dog biscuits, but have
quite a nice taste.   All the food that is left in the
vehicle.
   The men lunch off " issue biscuits " and bully beef.
   Almost as important as the food, the Major's servant

has contrived to find the wherewithal to eat it—one knife, one fork, and one spoon.

We squat down in a row in the ditch and pass the tins to one another in turn. The Major swallows his spoonful of Maconochie (which we have to eat cold) and passes the tin, and spoon, to the next man. The tin of potatoes follows down the line in the same way, accompanied by a fork. We are hungry. This is one of those occasions when there is no such thing as indifferent food. It all tastes grand. The tins go round till they are scraped clean. Three-quarters of an hour it takes.

It is a queer business, sitting here swallowing these last morsels of food in a ditch, devoid practically of personal belonging except the clothes we are wearing, just ourselves alone, with the enemy guns pounding in front of us, Dunkirk a roaring furnace behind, bombers roaring overhead, and the feeling within us of being detached from the rest of the universe, isolated in this flat, featureless plain under the wide, blazing sky.

" I'm dying for a drink," said the Major. " Anybody got any water ? "

Not a drop between the lot of us.

" Anything that's liquid will do," said the Major hopefully.

I go across to the mess vehicle, and after a lot of routing around return with one half-bottle of gin, one bottle of whisky, and one-quarter of a bottle of very acidulous red wine. And one cup !

The cup goes up and down the line as the tins had done previously.

" I can imagine how fine this would be with a splash of soda," says the A.C.P.O.

We frown on him.

We also had to do without the finale that would have rounded the lunch off nicely. Our tobacco had

226

long been exhausted. It was a pity, because there
happened to be a lull in the firing just then, even in
the bombing. And a pipe in that sudden spell of
comparative peace would have been very soothing.

*   *   *   *   *

Boyd decides he must have a post-prandial stroll.
He emerges from the ditch and walks off in front of
the Battery position in the direction of a small group
of wrecked houses half a mile away to the left.

To our surprise we suddenly see him galloping back
towards the Battery, mounted on a fine chestnut
gelding. It is a French army horse that has been
abandoned, like so many hundreds in the retreat's last
stages. Boyd has discovered it, saddle and bridle
complete, tethered behind one of the houses.

Boyd comes along just as if he has hounds in front
of him, clears the ditch in fine free style, pulls up at
our shelter, and dismounts.

" Ah ! " he exclaims luxuriously. " It's good to feel
a bit of horseflesh between your legs."

All of us burst into a laugh. The remark sounds
fearfully incongruous in the circumstances. Almost
like a great joke, though Boyd is serious enough. It
summons up the picture of a meet, on a soft November
morning. And could anything appear more fantastic
than that, here in this hell-of-a-corner where if anything was being hunted it was us, and the " kill "
seemed close at hand.

" What are you going to do with it, Boyd ? "
inquires the A.C.P.O. " Keep it to ride to the beach
on this evening ? If so, I'll ride pillion."

With this remark we are jerked back abruptly to
the realities of the present situation once more.

" I think not," replies Boyd, thoughtfully. " It
would be like murder. Down on the beach there'd
be nothing to feed it on. It would die for sure. I

227

shall leave it over there where I found it.   It'll stand
a better chance."

Boyd mounts again, and canters up and down the
Battery behind the guns in perfect cavalry style.
The gunners look on with delight and astonishment
at the unexpected equestrian display.   It is as good
as a circus to them.

After a quarter of an hour Boyd takes the horse
across the fields and returns to the ditch on foot.

" Best exercise in the world, old fellow," he says
to me, exuberantly.   " Just what I needed.   Keeps
you fit."

" Fit for what ? " I ask.

In the circumstances, not a happy remark.

*   *   *   *   *

Three p.m. . . . We are suddenly wrenched back
to our own grim business.   The whistle and flutter of
a shell overhead.   And it sounds pretty close.   Actually
it drops dead behind the Battery, about a hundred
yards away.   It is followed by another in the same
spot.

As we peer over the edge of the ditch we see white
smoke drifting towards us over the ground from the
places where the shells exploded.

Much to our discomfort we discover that these are
not two lone shells.   A third bursts a hundred yards
in front of the Battery, and another about a similar
distance behind.   The Germans are bracketing on us.
We've been spotted. . . .

We crouch down in the ditch.   Five of us in a
line under the tarpaulin cover.   Stuck out there, in
that bare, naked landscape, with nothing to hide or
shield us, even that tarpaulin gives us a sense of
protection, utterly misplaced though it may be.   We
feel that beneath it we personally are not quite so
starkly visible to enemy eyes. . . .

After the whistle of each shell we poke our heads up over the edge of the ditch for a look. Two more shells burst in quick succession only fifty yards in front. One lands fair and square on the Command Post Officer's truck, wrecking it and setting it ablaze. Gunners race over and put out the flames with fire-extinguishers from other vehicles.

Now, the C.P.O.'s truck bore his tactical sign "Y.I." And from this it became known throughout the Battery as "Y-Worry?" Somehow or other, this name had come to be painted on the truck. Certainly, it aptly reflected its owner's disposition.

But if the C.P.O. did not worry in a general sense, the sudden and shattering decease of his favourite truck saddened him a bit. He appeared quite pained when the A.C.P.O. cried cheerfully :

"Good ! That's one less vehicle we shall have to smash before we go."

And, oddly enough, having knocked "Y–Worry?" out of existence, the shelling immediately stopped. It was just like a personal message from the Germans to the C.P.O. that it was high time he started in to worry.

*   *   *   *   *

Three-thirty p.m. . . . Over come thirty more bombers. Dive-bombers and large two-engine Dorniers. The dive-bombers swoop down on the beaches. The Dorniers give hell to Dunkirk itself. Their bombs burst with a colossal "Whoom." The earth quivers under the blows. We can feel our Battery positions shake as if rocked by an earthquake. A dozen great plumes of black smoke and dust soar into the air at the same time, each at least a hundred feet tall. They hang down over Dunkirk from the blue skies like gigantic mourning pennons at the obsequies of some demi-god.

Back the bombers go, as soon as they have done their work. . . .

*   *   *   *   *

Four p.m. . . . Y–Battery breaks into life again after a short lull. The other regiments in the artillery ring round .Dunkirk continue firing spasmodically. Ever since daybreak some battery or other has been sending its shells crashing into the enemy masses that are being so stubbornly held on the line in front by our infantry.

The telephone rings in the Command Post in the ditch. It is R.H.Q. situated at the Wagon Lines, just behind us.

" Two harassing fire tasks for you. Give 'em a few bursts on and off at irregular intervals. I'll give you the map references of them. They are both at the cross-roads."

The Command Post Officer takes the map references and plots the targets on his artillery board, working out the switch, range, and angle of sight. He shouts out of the ditch for the Gun Post Officers to come to him, gives them the details and instructs them to fire five bursts of gun-fire at irregular intervals.

The G.P.O.'s hasten back to the guns.

" M–Troop. . . . Take Post . . ."
" L–Troop. . . . Take Post. . . ."
" N–Troop. . . . Take Post. . . ."
" Fresh target . . . H.E. 117. . . . Charge 3. . . . More 5 degrees. . . . Angle of sight, zero. . . . 10,000 (range). . . . Five rounds gun-fire at bursts. . . . Irregular intervals. . . ."

" FIRE. . . ."

In a few seconds our shells are pounding on the Germans concentrating over behind Adinkerke.

*   *   *   *   *

The Major also decides that it is about time we destroyed all the vehicles we are not going to utilise in getting away that night.

" I should get on with it at once," he says to me. " We'll leave five 15-cwts. That will be sufficient for our load. Destroy the remainder. . . . Oh, you might leave an extra 15-cwt. in case one gets knocked out."

I detail a couple of drivers to begin the work of destruction at once. First the radiators are drained, and the engines set running to seize them up. A couple of hefty blows with the pick-axe finish off the radiators. After the tyres are deflated they are cut and slashed to ribbons. All the glass is smashed and the steering wheels broken. When the engines have stopped the sledge-hammers get to work, smashing plugs, magneto and carburettor.

It is an orgy of ruin and enforced waste. A pitiable proceeding. . . .

The two drivers, swinging their sledge-hammers like professional navvies, slaughter half a dozen cars in an hour. That, considering the scorching heat, means real work. . They wipe off their perspiration and stand back to view their devastation with a grim admiration.

I feel that another link binding me to the battle has been broken. . . .

Among the drivers' victims is my own truck with the perforated windscreen (thirteen machine-gun bullet holes) that, during those far-off days at Arras, I had installed as my mascot for as long as the War lasted. You may remember that I had toyed with the idea of taking my mascot back to England with me on my next leave. An uneasy sensation took hold of me at the thought of the sledgehammer shattering that glass. It had been a most hard-working mascot in its time. Would it understand the necessity

231

for its ill-treatment ?   Or would it bear me a
grudge ? . . .

    *   *   *   *   *

Six p.m. . . . Another quiet spell of the guns.
And another sign that our time is now drawing
near.

The Number Ones take the first step in their preparations for blowing up the guns.   They attach a 50-yards
length of signal wire to the trigger lever of each gun.

That is all for the present.   But the significance of
the simple act reaches far beyond its routine formality.
Like a judge putting on the Black Cap. . . .

    *   *   *   *   *

Seven p.m. . . . The bombers over again.   This
time they are caught by our fighter patrols who
plummet down from the evening sky on their prey.
In a twinkle of an eye three Germans are brought
down, and another couple limp homeward trailing tails
of black smoke.   The remainder flee east as fast as
their engines can take them.

A most successful interception, this.   The beaches
are saved entirely, and Dunkirk itself only gets one or
two bombs.

    *   *   *   *   *

Eight p.m. . . . And now, with only two and a
half more hours to go, we begin to feel the strain.
And to show signs of it.   Hitherto, our attitude has
been one of patient resignation.   When dawn broke,
10.30 p.m. seemed some far-off fabulous time.   So
fabulous indeed, that it appeared to have little con-
nection with the immediate realities that were ours.
A date in a different era.   We had no particular
expectation that we should ever make it.   A complete

day in front of us. A day consisting of long long
hours, every minute of which held for us all the direful
possibilities of the Unknown.   In face of this it would
have been foolish of us to look upon 10.30 p.m. as in
any way belonging to us. So we didn't. We simply
embedded ourselves in the moment that happened to
be with us. That, at least, was ours to grip on to and
to act in. We did not think of dying. And we did
not think of living. We had some Fate or other
hovering very near to us and we were resigned to it.

But 10.30 p.m. looked at from 8.0 p.m. was a very
different matter.   Here was an hour almost within our
grasp. One that we might reasonably expect to
assume possession of.

We have a chance after all. . . .

And as the minutes pass we undergo a change. We
begin to think much more of life than at any time
since the Invasion. Life looms up large in front of us
on that sinister plain outside Dunkirk. And life looks
sweet. We begin to hope that the enemy will not
discover us. We feel it would be tragic if anything
happened now. Tragic, after existing through all
those ages since dawn.

There are visible signs of this alteration in us. When
we hear a shell coming we adopt no half-measures to
get out of its way. Odd bits of shell fragments have
been hissing round us for hours, coming from nowhere
in particular, some from our own ack-ack guns.
Hitherto we haven't bothered much about them. But
now we develop a tendency to fling ourselves flat on
the ground at the merest sound. No one exhibits the
slightest shame. There is no room among us for
false heroics. Any idea of courting unnecessary
danger is miles from us. Except when actually firing
no one budges an inch from the ditch without very
powerful reasons. If ten chestnut stallions had come
along at that moment I doubt if they would have

aroused any appetite in Boyd for a ride.   Yes, 8.0 p.m.
is a very different thing from 3.0 p.m. with all of
us. . . .

We begin to ponder on the beaches—on all that we
have heard of the shambles and the slaughter.   This,
now, has a near and vital interest for us.   Soon we
shall be concerned in it ourselves.   Again we confront
that menacing paradox : the Gate of Deadly Danger
opening to the Road to Safety.   We still have to face
the Worst before we can win the Best.   Shall we win
it ?   And how many of us ?

Other signs are manifest of the last-hour strain.
We grow very touchy, and answer in monosyllables.
Orders are given snappily.   We find ourselves looking
at one another without speaking. . . .

A cigarette would relieve the tension but there isn't
one in the Battery. . . .

So would a stroll.   But no one fancies the risk.   We
all prefer the tension. . . .

In one short, heartfelt utterance of three words
the C.P.O. expresses the sentiments of the entire
Battery. . . .

" Roll on, Time ! "

*   *   *   *   *

Eight-thirty p.m. . . .   Our throats are parched.
We have nothing to drink.   And haven't had, for
hours.   Nothing to eat, also, except biscuits.   These
are dry, the evening is hot and airless—especially
under the tarpaulin—and so our thirst increases.

Our guns, and the other rearguard batteries continue firing in spasmodic bursts.   All along the line in
front, where our infantry are locked in their struggle
with the Germans, the rattle of machine-gun fire is
incessant, punctuated every now and then by the deep
boom of the enemy artillery.   Just behind us the
factory is still burning.   It has been one big blaze

since dawn. The black pall of Dunkirk is still the
backcloth of our little drama.

Twilight begins to fall over the flat naked country-
side stretching before us in the direction of the front
line. The land appears peculiarly deserted, unin-
habited, isolated. There is hardly a single sign of
movement to be seen anywhere. No troops on the
roads at all. Just occasionally an ambulance full of
wounded appears in the distance, travelling down one
of the roads leading to Dunkirk. The Red Cross on
the white circle seems startlingly vivid. An invitation to attack, I think, remembering the dozens of
ambulances I have seen riddled with machine-gun
bullets.

*   *   *   *   *   *

Nine-thirty p.m. . . . Getting dark now. . . .
Preparations for our final exit move another step forward. All ammunition considered surplus to the
requirements of the next hour is to be destroyed.

" Tell the Troops to do it straightaway," say the
Major. " Better take the cordite bags out of the
cartridge cases, open the bags and scatter the stuff
over the ground. A hundred yards behind the guns.
Take the shells over to the canal and drop them into
the water. Fire off the primers in the cartridge cases
by putting them in the gun."

So now, in the gathering gloom, men like sowers
move indistinctly in the field behind the guns. And
the seed they are sowing is cordite. If any German
lies down in that field for a quiet smoke and throws
away a lighted match he will get the shock of his life.
An instant sheet of flame will envelop him.

Another line of dimly-seen men trudge backwards
and forwards between the guns and the canal, a
25-pounder shell tucked under each arm . . .

The gunners have a splendid time firing off the

primers. They go back to their toy-soldiering days. Each primer explodes with a tiny report which echoes in the big empty barrel of the gun with a musical " Ping."

Over at the Wagon Lines all the tractors and trailers have been smashed.

The Battery is now in an advanced state of liquidation . . .

*　　　*　　　*　　　*　　　*

Ten-fifteen p.m.—It has all become very silent. Even the German firing has died down . . . Like the lull before a great event. The sudden hush gets on our nerves. Ominous. Surely nothing is going to happen to stop us now. We keep glancing at our wrist-watches . . . Every minute or so. Not a word is spoken.

Suddenly the telephone back to R.H.Q. at the Wagon Lines tinkles. The Major picks it up, listens a moment or two, and then turns to us.

" That was R.H.Q.," he says quietly. " We've got to stop in action till eleven."

We looked at one another in silence. It was a shocking disappointment. Too big for words. Another half-hour ! That was like an eternity under present conditions. Anything could happen in half an hour. The feeling that we are going to be cheated after all seizes upon us.

*　　　*　　　*　　　*　　　*

Ten-forty-five p.m.—The Major gives the order for the five vehicles that are to convey us away, to be collected and drawn up about 400 yards to the right flank of the Battery position.

*　　　*　　　*　　　*　　　*

Ten-fifty-five p.m.—The Major looks at his watch.

" Time, now," he says curtly. " Prepare the guns for demolition."

The Troop-Commanders go off to supervise. It is very dark, now. The backcloth has changed. No longer Dunkirk the pall, but Dunkirk the angry, red-hot, glowing cinder. And above it the menacing glare in the sky.

All the gunners except the Number Ones and one man for each gun are ordered to the vehicles on the flank of the Battery, where they sit waiting.

They depart laden with valuable instruments which we still hope to salve. Each gunner is entrusted with a piece of equipment, a dial sight, a field clinometer, an angle-of-sight clinometer. Parts of the survey staff that had remained behind are given the director-heads. Such valuable things are not lightly to be destroyed, even in this emergency.

Lest we have to spend a day on the beach and dig-in, all available picks and spades are taken. The Bren gunners keep their Bren-gun and anti-tank rifles in case we are attacked.

The N.C.O. in charge of Signals makes a last tour round, smashing telephones, director stands, artillery boards, and wireless sets.

*   *   *   *   *

A gunner picks up a shell, takes the fuse-cap off, and slides it tenderly down the muzzle of the gun towards the breech. Then, very deliberately and care-fully he puts another shell in the breech. Then a charge, in the normal way. On the ground near the breech he deposits another charge in case of mis-fire.

It is all carried out very quietly and calmly under the watchful eye of the Troop-Commanders and the Number Ones The bitterest humiliation that can befall a battery in war is about to befall Y–Battery.

Yet the preparations go on, methodical, unemotional.

*   *   *   *   *

At last the moment has arrived. The Troop-Commanders report to the Major.

" Our guns are ready for demolition."

" Right-o," says the Major. " Get off to the vehicles."

Everybody retires to the right flank of the Battery except the Number Ones who proceed to the ends of the wires attached to the trigger levers of the guns, fifty yards away. We can discern them standing there in the darkness, motionless, like sentinels . . . All in a line.

Suddenly on the left of the line appears the shadowy figure of the Major. He walks up to the first Number One who hands him the end of the wire. There is the faintest breath of a pause. Then the Major pulls with a jerk.

Immediately a shattering explosion, and a blinding white flash where the gun stood . . .

The Major is on his way to the next . . .

As he draws nearer to us we lie flat on the ground by the vehicles to avoid the danger of flying metal. We count the explosions. One . . . two . . three . . . four . . . five . . . six . . . seven . . .

Each is like a heart-stab. Each explosion might be a volley fired over the grave of a departed friend. Each blinding flash a funeral pyre . . .

We are losing our guns. And to a gunner, his guns are his colours. Had it been left to us we'd have dragged those guns down to the very beach. And on to the boat, if possible.

What a passing ! Over all, the thick, black mantle of the foreboding night. And Dunkirk glaring to us its angry invitation . . .

*   *   *   *   *

We count the last explosion. It is finished. Out of the darkness steps the Major.

" Get mounted. Let's go," he says abruptly.

He turns to me as he passes.

" It's a bloody shame we had to do that," he says.

XX—On the Beaches

The fifty of us divided ourselves among the five vehicles. We moved off in the darkness, not the faintest flicker of a tail-light showing. Not a word was spoken. It was as if we were saving our breath for the final ordeal. We each had our own urgent thoughts to occupy us. Our faces were at last turned towards that smoking furnace, for so many long hours our grim threatening backcloth. In a short while we should penetrate it. We should march into those red, devouring jaws. What should we see ? What would happen to us ? We were gripped by a fearful fascination.

In the pitch blackness we crawled across the field to the pavé road. Not a soul was to be seen. The place was deserted except for our own trucks. There was no moon, though a few stars shone in a deep indigo sky. The summer lightning still flashed intermittently along the horizon towards the east where the German guns continued active. And, of course, we had the dreadful beacon of Dunkirk in front of us. Our progress was hardly more than a walking pace. It was impossible, dangerous indeed, to move faster. The road was strewn with the wreckage of the last stages of the retreat—trucks, lorries, equipment. We were continually pulling up to avoid them. And when we did so we usually found ourselves bumping into shell holes. Stray flashes and explosions, some near, some not so near, kept us in a state of wakefulness, worn-out though we were.

After ten minutes we turned off the road to the

right, towards Malo-les-Bains, which to Dunkirk is
as Hove to Brighton.   A blinding flash and a tremendous explosion met us.   I was riding in the front of
the first truck and the concussion hit me in the chest
with the full force of a heavy-weight punch, knocking
me backwards.   The sergeant driving beside me was
temporarily blinded.   He was a man who knew not
fear, and his unshakable calm was proverbial in the
Battery.   But he was ruffled all right this time.

"Christ Almighty!   What   was   that?"   he   exclaimed.

These were the first words spoken since we started
our journey.

It may have been an enemy shell, or possibly some
French gun that had just fired on top of us in the
darkness.   We did not stop to inquire.   As soon as
the stunning effect passed off we pushed on, fearful
lest the next shell might get us.

Eventually we arrived at the spot on this side of
the last canal separating us from the sea, where we
had to abandon the vehicles.   They were smashed up
in the darkness and pushed into the canal.   The men
formed up by the roadside and the roll was called for
the last time.   A weird scene, the Troop sergeant-
majors calling out the names of the gunners in loud
whispers, and ticking them off on their lists by torch-
light as the answers came back out of the darkness,
from nowhere it seemed.

"All present and correct, sir."

And once more the fifty of us started off, this time
on foot, formed-up in threes, the Major and I walking
at the head of the column.   To our great joy we discovered that the bridge spanning the canal had not
been smashed.   Once over it, and another obstacle
between us and the Unknown had been passed.   We
continued towards Malo-les-Bains, crossing the railway,
and marching through the ruined street of Rosendaal

whose skeleton walls stood around us like the ruins of some bygone civilisation. The only sound was the crunching of the broken glass under our feet, as if we were marching over hard ice-crystals on a winter's day. Mysterious shadows flitted about the streets, in and out of broken doorways, and disappearing silently round corners. They were stray inhabitants who had been cut-off by the swift march of events and were living in cellars. And a few looters. And, probably, a few spies. The German gun-fire was now incessant, the flash of the explosions continually lighting up the scene for a second or two on every side of us.

Now we were no longer alone. We began to meet little batches of our infantry marching in the same direction. Often as we approached we would be hailed out of the darkness :

" Is that A–Company, King's Own Scottish Borderers ? . . ." Or the name of some other unit would be shouted. These were bits of the rearguard coming back, and marching still in good formation down to the beaches.

The road became very narrow, and adding to the difficulties of getting along, the troops were harassed by an incessant hooting from behind, which after a time got on everybody's nerves more than the shell-fire. Finally, we halted to discover what the fuss was about. A crowd of panic-stricken French poilus were trying to drive their lorries in the darkness right through our marching infantry, knocking them to right and left off the road into the ditches. Angry words passed. There seemed great likelihood that a fight would take place. Fortunately, at the last moment the French drivers thought better of it, and fell in behind the troops. It was high time, too. We were just in the mood to shoot if necessary. They followed behind us at a marching pace for some time till they turned off down another road.

We were now in the region of the dunes, which rose like humps of a deeper darkness. And these in their turn were dotted with the still blacker shapes of abandoned vehicles, half-sunk in the sand, fantastic twisted shapes of burned-out skeletons, and crazy-looking wreckage that had been heaped up in extraordinary piles by the explosions of bombs. All these black shapes were silhouetted against the angry red glare in the sky, which reflected down on us the agony of burning Dunkirk.

Slowly we picked our way between the wreckage, sinking ankle-deep in the loose sand, until we reached the gaunt skeletons of what had once been the houses on the promenade. The whole front was one long continuous line of blazing buildings, a high wall of fire, roaring and darting in tongues of flame, with the smoke pouring upwards and disappearing in the blackness of the sky above the roof-tops. Out seawards the darkness was as thick and smooth as black velvet, except for now and again when the shape of a sunken destroyer or paddle-steamer made a slight thickening on its impenetrable surface. Facing us, the great black wall of the Mole stretched from the beach far out into sea, the end of it almost invisible to us. The Mole had an astounding, terrifying background of giant flames leaping a hundred feet into the air from blazing oil tanks. At the shore end of the Mole stood an obelisk, and the high explosive shells burst around it with monotonous regularity.

Along the promenade, in parties of fifty, the remnants of practically all the last regiments were wearily trudging along. There was no singing, and very little talk. Everyone was far too exhausted to waste breath. Occasionally out of the darkness came a sudden shout :

" A–Company, Green Howards. . . ."
" C–Company, East Yorks. . . ."

These shouts came either from stragglers trying to find lost units, or guides on the look-out for the parties they were to lead on to the Mole for evacuation.

The tide was out. Over the wide stretch of sand could be dimly discerned little oblong masses of soldiers, moving in platoons and orderly groups down towards the edge of the sea. Now and again you would hear a shout :

" Alf, where are you ? " . . ."

" Let's hear from you, Bill. . . ."

" Over this way, George. . . ."

It was none too easy to keep contact with one's friends in the darkness, and amid so many little masses of moving men, all looking very much alike. If you stopped for a few seconds to look behind the chances were you attached yourself to some entirely different unit.

From the margin of the sea, at fairly wide intervals, three long thin black lines protruded into the water, conveying the effect of low wooden breakwaters. These were lines of men, standing in pairs behind one another far out into the water, waiting in queues till boats arrived to transport them a score or so at a time, to the steamers and warships that were filling up with the last survivors. The queues stood there, fixed and almost as regular as if ruled. No bunching, no pushing, Nothing like the mix-up to be seen at the turnstiles when a crowd is going into a football match. Much more orderly, even, than a waiting theatre queue.

About this time, afraid that some of our own men might be tailing off, I began shouting : " 2004th Field Regiment . . . 2004th Field Regiment . . ." We were also having difficulty in finding our report centre.

" I wonder where this blasted report centre is," said the Major. " Give another shout. If they hear us they can shout back instructions and tell us what to do."

So from this point I went along shouting. But the report centre failed to materialise, and soon we decided that hanging about any longer on the promenade looking for it might prove disastrous. Heavy shells commenced crashing into the tops of the ruined buildings along the promenade, bringing down heaps of brick and masonry almost on our heads.

" It'll be healthier on the beach," said the Major.

A group of dead and dying soldiers on the path in front of us quickened our desire to quit the promenade. Stepping over the bodies we marched down the slope on to the dark beach. Dunkirk front was now a lurid study in red and black ; flames, smoke, and the night itself all mingling together to compose a frightful panorama of death and destruction. Red and black, all the time, except for an occasional flash of white low in the sky miles away to the left and right where big shells from coastal defence guns at Calais and Nieuport were being hurled into the town.

Down on the beach you immediately felt yourself surrounded by a deadly evil atmosphere. A horrible stench of blood and mutilated flesh pervaded the place. There was no escape from it. Not a breath of air was blowing to dissipate the appalling odour that arose from the dead bodies that had been lying on the sand, in some cases for several days. We might have been walking through a slaughter-house on a hot day. The darkness, which hid some of the sights of horror from our eyes, seemed to thicken this dreadful stench. It created the impression that death was hovering around, very near at hand.

We set our faces in the direction of the sea, quickening our pace to pass through the belt of this nauseating miasma as soon as possible.

" Water . . . Water . . ." groaned a voice from the ground just in front of us.

It was a wounded infantryman. He had been hit

so badly that there was no hope for him. Our water-bottles had long been empty, but by carefully draining them all into one we managed to collect a mouthful or two. A sergeant knelt down beside the dying man and held the bottle to his lips. Then we proceeded on our way, leaving the bottle with the last few drains in it near the poor fellow's hand so that he could moisten his lips from time to time.

On either side, scattered over the sand in all sorts of positions, were the dark shapes of dead and dying men, sometimes alone, sometimes in twos and threes. Every now and then we had to pull ourselves up sharply in the darkness to avoid falling over a wooden cross erected by comrades on the spot where some soldier had been buried. No assistance that availed anything could be given to these dying men. The living themselves had nothing to offer them. They just pressed forward to the sea, hoping that the same fate would not be theirs. And still it remained a gamble all the time whether that sea, close though it was, would be reached in safety. Splinters from bursting shells were continually whizzing through the air, and occasionally a man in one of the plodding groups would fall with a groan.

The darkness, as I have said, was mercifully saving us from many a spectacle of horror. Moreover it was saving us from the additional danger of bombing. Seeing as much as we did see gave us every reason for thanking God that we had come down to the beach at night, and not in the daytime. There was still another dread haunting us. Should we be able to get off the beach before dawn discovered us, and those waves of German bombers that we had watched the previous day diving over Dunkirk had us for a target ?

" I'm not too comfortable in my mind about things," Boyd muttered to me as we proceeded along.

Comfortable ! Were any of us ?

I stepped over the corpse of a man who had been killed just as he was trying to take cover in a shallow depression he had evidently been frantically digging when the bombers appeared. He had flung himself forward flat on his face towards it, and half his body only lay in the saucer-like grave. The dry sand was slipping down from the sides in little streams, gradually burying his head.

Comfortable in my mind ? I should think not. If I had been inclined to laugh at anything just then, it would have been at Boyd's colossal understatement.

On we trudged, occasionally passing a slightly wounded man who limped along supported by a comrade on either side. All the time shouts of people identifying one another broke the silence. I, too, was now continually shouting : " 2004th Field Regiment. . . . 2004th Field Regiment. . . ."

We came at last to the water's edge, where the wreck of a dive bomber, standing up on its nose like a war memorial, bore somewhat of the aspect of a happy augury. Along the margin of the sea, a little way out, could be distinguished at intervals the hulls of bombed rescue vessels—tugs, drifters, a destroyer, a hospital ship, and several lifeboats.

" We'll have a rest here," said the Major. And the suggestion was very welcome to all of us. Particularly so to me, for I had marched the whole of the way in my greatcoat, which I was determined not to lose if I could possibly save it. The A.C.P.O. was similarly burdened, and had other woes, of which more anon. The C.P.O. was giving, for some reason I have never quite been able to fathom, a very creditable impression of a padre on tour. It may have been the haversack slung across his shoulders. It may have been his big walking-stick. A bit of a mystery, but there it was. The Major, greatly daring, had encumbered himself with a suit-case. Of which, also, more anon.

247

We were now close to the Mole on the beach. While we rested Boyd and the C.P.O. decided to walk a little farther on, in a last attempt to discover something about our report centre. The A.C.P.O. leaned wearily against me.

" Do you know," he said, in an almost heart-broken tone, " I think I shall have to part with Theo the Dolite after all. I hate to admit it, but he's too much for me."

I found nothing comic in the A.C.P.O.'s grief. I understood what he was suffering. The A.C.P.O. had developed a fond affection for the Battery's theodolite, a very valuable instrument. No other theodolite in the army could stand up against this, in the A.C.P.O.'s estimation. He had bestowed on it a pet name, Theo the Dolite, and never referred to it in any other terms. When the Battery was liquidated he had taken Theo under his protection, determined at all costs that it should not be left behind. No, not if he had to carry it all the way to England himself. Which was a valiant decision, in the circumstances. For the theodolite represented the weight of a well-filled suit-case.

" I'm sorry, very sorry, old fellow," I said. " But you've done your best."

" Yes. I can't go on with it," he replied mournfully.

He rose, and I watched him walk over to the water's edge, pause for a second or two, and then drop Theo the Dolite into the water. He let it fall gently so that it made hardly a splash. It was too dark to see his face when he returned, but it would never surprise me to learn that he had tears in his eyes.

In a quarter of an hour Boyd and the C.P.O. returned. They had had no luck.

" In any case," said the Major, " I don't like the look of the Mole. You saw the shelling going on at the land end. They know it's packed with troops

248

waiting to be taken off. It's sure to get a bad time."

To all of which we heartily agreed.

" Shall we try to get off from the beach ? " said the Major. " Wade into the water, and take our chance in one of the queues ? That's my idea."

No one had any criticism of this proposal to offer. It fitted in with the fears and desires of each one of us. After another five minutes' rest we stood up, fell-in the men, and led them down to the water's edge.

We tacked ourselves on to the rear of the smallest of the three queues, the head of which was already standing in water up to the waist. Half an hour passed. Suddenly a small rowing boat appeared. The head of the queue clambered in and were rowed away into the blackness. We moved forward, and the water rose to our waists.

Our only thoughts now, were to get on a boat. Along the entire queue not a word was spoken. The men just stood there silently staring into the darkness, praying that a boat would soon appear, and fearing that it would not. Heads and shoulders only showing above the water. Fixed, immovable, as though chained there. It was, in fact, practically impossible to move, even from one foot to another. The dead-weight of waterlogged boots and sodden clothes pinned one down. My breeches seemed to be ballooned out with water as heavy as mercury. I was filled with a dread that when the time did come I should be unable to move. Every now and then as we stood there rooted in the sea, a slight swell stirred the surface and the water rose to my chest, and up to the necks of the shorter men. We thanked Heaven that the night was calm. Had there been a strong breeze blowing the swell would have swamped us and, I suppose, many of us would have been drowned, for we were too exhausted to make any struggle against a heavy sea.

We glued our eyes in the direction whence was to come our salvation. Another lifeboat appeared but it halted at the head of the queue on our right. Enviously we watched as it filled up.

" Not too many on one side or you'll have her over," came the cry.

Off went the boat, and again we resumed our vigil. Minutes became hours ; and hours an eternity. After a long while we were attacked by a horrible dread that there would not be any more boats. That we should stand there half submerged in water through-out the night, and then, after all, have to spend the day on the beach. A leaden depression seized us, and our hearts became as heavy as our water-logged bodies. The weariness of the wait was appalling. Try as we could we found it impossible to keep our eyes open. Half of us were asleep standing up. And every one of us kept waking with a start out of the sort of coma that descended on us.

The A.C.P.O., standing beside me, suddenly turned his head towards me and nodded significantly. It was as if he read the thought that was passing in my own mind. I nodded back. The time had come for another sacrifice.

The A.C.P.O. and I had indulged ourselves in two expensive rain-proof map cases. We took great pride in these possessions, and clung on to them to the end. And now the end had come. In our exhausted state they seemed to weigh a ton. We hadn't the strength to carry them another minute.

We looked at one another mournfully, the A.C.P.O. and I. Then simultaneously we tossed our burdens into the water, without saying a word. They floated off, half-submerged, till they were swallowed up in the darkness. Almost at the same moment I heard a

splash behind me. Half-turning I was just in time
to see the Major's suit-case disappear beneath the
water. He, too, had had to give in. And now,
without the consciousness of the struggle to retain it
to keep him awake, he immediately closed his eyes
and began to fall asleep.

During all this time the German shells continued to
rain upon the town. Stray hot splinters flew round
our heads, hissing as they fell into the water. Still
Dunkirk showed its long flaming front behind us.
The red glare in the sky extended over us. Along
the Mole, a quarter of a mile to our left crept the tiny
figures of the soldiers being evacuated by the ships.
Little black figures, silhouetted against red fire.

XXI—THE FINEST SIGHT IN THE WORLD

Ages passed—ages as one measured time in those fateful minutes. We began to give up hope of a boat. Our tired eyes hurt from straining to pierce the darkness.

Suddenly out of the blackness, rather ghostly, swam a white shape which materialised into a ship's lifeboat, towed by a motor-boat. It moved towards us and came to a stop twenty yards in front of the head of our queue.

" Hi ! Hi ! " we all hailed, dreading they hadn't seen us.

" Ahoy ! Ahoy ! " came the lusty response.

" Come in closer," we shouted.

" We can't. It's unsafe. Might upset the boat."

But they risked a few more yards.

There was a slight hesitation at the head of the queue. As I have said, the water already stood above our waists. So fearful was I that the boat might move off and leave us that I struggled to the head of the queue and waded forward crying : " Come on the 2004th ! " That set everyone moving, and soon I was caught up and passed.

Higher rose the water every step we took. Soon it reached my armpits, and was lapping the chins of the shorter men. The blind urge to safety drove us on whether we could swim or not. Our feet just maintained contact with the bottom by the time we reached the side of the boat.

Four sailors in tin-hats began hoisting the soldiers out of the water. It was no simple task. Half the men were so weary and exhausted that they lacked

252

strength to climb into the boat unaided. The sailors judged the situation perfectly, as being one for rough words, threats, and bullying methods. The only spur sufficient to rouse our worn-out bodies to one last supreme effort.

" Come on, you bastards. . . ."

" Wake up, blast you. . . ."

" Get a move on, Dopey. . . ."

The gunwale of the lifeboat stood three feet above the surface of the water. Reaching up, I could just grasp it with the tips of my fingers. When I tried to haul myself up I couldn't move an inch. The weight of my waterlogged clothes, especially my cherished greatcoat, beat me completely, desperately though I fought. I might have been a sack of lead. A great dread of being left behind seized me.

Two powerful hands reached over the gunwale and fastened themselves into my arm-pits. Another pair of hands stretched down and hooked-on to the belt at the back of my great-coat. Before I had time to realise it I was pulled up and pitched head-first into the bottom of the boat.

" Come on, you b——. Get up and help the others in," shouted a sailor, as I hit the planks with a gasp.

It was all rough medicine. But the right medicine for the moment.

The boat was now getting crowded. I wondered who else of our party had made it. I shouted the Major's name. There was no reply. " Boyd," I shouted, and from somewhere in the darkness he answered. The A.C.P.O. replied : " Here I am " from my very elbow. I continued shouting names of men. The good proportion of responses gladdened me.

The moment came when the lifeboat could not hold another soul.

" Carry on, Mr. Jolly. Carry on," cried the sailor at our helm to someone in the motor-boat.

And we got under weigh, leaving the rest of the queue behind to await the next boat.

From the very instant I landed on my head in that lifeboat a great burden of responsibility seemed to fall from my shoulders. A queer sense of freedom took possession of me. All the accumulated strain of the last few hours, of the last day or so, vanished. I felt that my job was over. Anything else that remained to be done was the Navy's business. I was in their hands, and had nothing more to worry about. There and then, on that dark and sinister sea, an indescribable sense of luxurious contentment enveloped me.

Again the hearty voice of our helmsman :

" Little bit more to the left, Mr. Jolly. Little bit more to the left. Or we'll hit her in the backside."

The unseen Mr. Jolly so contrived as to avoid this disaster, and the grey flank of H.M. *Medway Queen*, paddle-steamer, loomed in front of us, her shadowy decks already packed with troops from the beaches. In a minute or two our boatload was submerged in the crowd.

Boyd, the A.C.P.O. and myself managed to keep together, and a little later who should appear but the Major.

" Pleased to see you got in, Major," I said. " I called your name, but there was no answer."

" Who else got away ? "

I gave him all the names I had.

" By the way," he said, " I've just been informed that our battery was the last battery in the B.E.F. to come out of action."

For some while now, ever since I entered the life-boat, I had forgotten Dunkirk. Such thoughts as I did possess were monopolised by England. The Major's words swung my mind back again for a moment. I gazed beyond the stern of the vessel, back to that dreadful strip of shore from which I had

254

been snatched to safety. There it was. One long line of flame on the horizon, suffusing the dark sky with its dull red, angry glare. Tortured, martyred Dunkirk. . . .

" Let's go down to the ward-room," said the Major, and passing stretcher-loads of wounded we stumbled along to a small compartment, thick with officers, and even thicker with an air you could cut with a knife. They were sitting around smoking ship's cigarettes, and munching ship's chocolate and meat sandwiches. Of the sixty or so, most were in various stages of dishevelment. One had nothing on except a towel ; another wore clothes borrowed from a seaman. A Guard's staff officer with a large gash in his tin helmet informed me that he had been on the beach for seven complete days organising the embarkation.

" By George ! " exclaimed the Major in the middle of this fog. " How I could do with a drink."

Somebody overheard and handed him a water-bottle. The Major put it gratefully to his lips and, thinking it was water, tossed his head back to take a long draught. He jerked his head back again even quicker, coughing and spluttering. It was rum.

The A.C.P.O. and I sat squeezed together on the settee that ran along the whole length of the ward-room, his head pillowed on my chest, mine on his shoulder. In the hot atmosphere our sopping clothes already emitted quite respectable clouds of steam. Irresistible drowsiness seized us.

Dimly-heard scraps of the conversations going on around penetrated my doze.

" Was he at Arras ? . . ."

" Wish I could get my socks off. . . ."

Got a cigarette, old boy ? . . ."

The 1st Battalion took a bad knock. . . ."

And then it was the A.C.P.O.'s voice speaking peevishly, as it seemed, from my own chest :

255

" You needn't have put your foot in my eye when I was helping you into the boat. . . ."

And Boyd in protest: " Could I help my foot slipping ? . . ."

Then no more voices.

*   *   *   *   *

" We're going into harbour ! "

Not one voice, but the whole wardroom seemed to be shouting it.

The A.C.P.O. and I woke with a combined jerk. Everyone was streaming towards the deck in a great bustle and commotion. We jammed on our tin-hats and pushed our way along with them.

It was a beautiful sunny June morning. Not a speck of cloud in the blue sky. And there in the pearly light that a slight haze created we saw the finest sight in the world.

" Ramsgate ! " I exclaimed.

" England," murmured the A.C.P.O.

" And beds to sleep in ! " I said.

THE END